THE DEBUTANTE BALL

BETH HENLEY

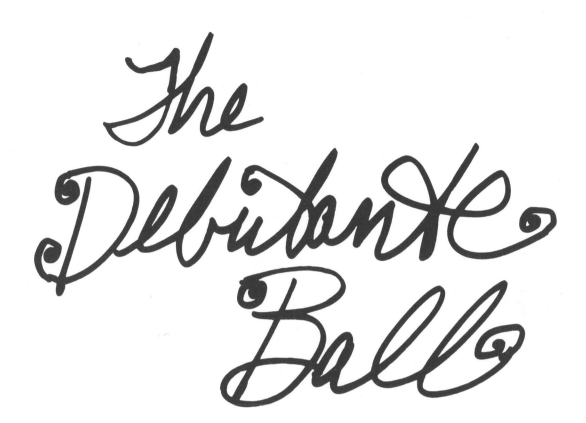

The Debutante Ball

with art by
Lynn Green Root

University Press of Mississippi   **Jackson and London**

Cataloging-in-Publication data appear on page 98.

Designed by John A. Langston

Printed in Singapore by Eurasia Press

The Debutante Ball was originally produced by South Coast Repertory. New York Premiere by The Manhattan Theatre Club on April 26, 1988

Funding for this book was provided in part by a grant from the Mississippi Arts Commission.

with love, to **GILBERT PARKER**
for your eternal support

CONTENTS

Illustrations   ix

Preface *by Beth Henley*   xi

The Debutante Ball

      Act I   3

      Act II   59

ILLUSTRATIONS

"Well, first I thought it was some wild child crying."   7

"Lord in heaven, what a luxurious bathroom."   10

Brighton is a very well-dressed, proper young man.   14

"Teddy, why are you wearing socks on your hands?"   18

"Teddy! Where are you, my darling child? My wondrous salvation?
Your debutante bouquet has arrived."   21

"Why, I had the florist make up nine different rose bouquets before
I approved the one that was exactly exquisitely right for your
ensemble."   24

Hank steps on Teddy's foot.   32

Teddy enters from her room. She wears her debutante's gown, a white
satin cape, silver slippers and carries a glittering evening bag.   41

Teddy puts roll-on deodorant behind her knees.   44

Hank   48

"Look, one cheese knife."   60

"I glanced over and saw his left arm was cut off right above the elbow."   62

"I used to write secrets in jars and bury the jars outside in the dirt."   65

"Teddy made her first bow with her gown pulled up over her head and two feet of toilet paper stuck to her slipper."   66

"I discovered her hairpiece floating in the punch bowl."   70

"IT'S RED . . . IT'S RED JUST LIKE YOUR LIPS."   78

"I can't get involved with you people no more."   82

PREFACE

The Debutante Ball, one of my stranger plays, evolved over a number of years. I first conceived of the play in the spring of 1982 but, because of a number of other commitments, was forced to put it aside for months at a time. I kept coming back to it, though, and found myself working on it, in fits and starts, for almost two years.

I was finally able to settle down in the winter of 1984 to try to put all the pieces together. I had a stack of spiral notebooks, notecards, cocktail napkins, and theater stubs all scrawled with cryptic notes, and a clear sense of the play's central images. Unfortunately, I had just returned from New York City where my latest play, *The Wake of Jamey Foster,* had opened and closed in one week, after an onslaught of savage reviews. The consensus was that *The Wake* was indulgent, excessive, even grotesque. I remember wondering what kind of life this new play—which had an onstage miscarriage as its climax and a fifty-two-year-old nude woman covered with psoriasis (sitting in a bathtub) as its final image—would have.

I finished *The Debutante Ball* in the late spring of 1984 and gave it to my theatrical agent, Gilbert Parker. Gilbert was supportive but concerned: "Do you have to have the bathroom onstage? Do we have to see the ladies shaving under their arms?" I assured him that, yes, this was a play about facades and secrets and suppressions and longings and that I wanted my characters to be seen as animals fighting to pluck and spray and shave away their true natures—adorning themselves with lies. Gilbert acquiesced and said he'd send the play out. He just hoped that the deaf community wouldn't picket.

The deaf community picket?

Gilbert said that the deaf character I'd written was an illiterate lesbian who behaved like a fool and that certainly in the "underpants" scene I'd gone too far. I argued that not all deaf people had to be portrayed as spunky, smart, and well groomed, and that, anyway, I'd written the part with Phyliss Frelich (a brilliant actress whom I had seen in *Children of a Lesser God*) in mind. Furthermore, I was certain that an actress of her caliber could handle both the comedy and the pathos in the so-called "underpants" scene.

With no further arguments, Gilbert decided to send the play out and give it a whirl. I waited and waited. No positive responses. Just a steady stream of polite rejections. Finally, some time later, Gilbert called and wanted to know if I was sitting down. I told him that after twenty-eight rejections, I was lying down. Then, the news: The South Coast Repertory Theater wanted to do *The Debutante Ball* in their spring slot and they wanted to put it on the main stage.

In the spring of 1986 we were off and running. I was ecstatic when Phyliss Frelich read the play and consented to be part of the company. I had a wonderful cast and a director I believed in. The only problem was the script. It rambled and stumbled—alternately astonishing and appalling. The first preview was so painful that I left the auditorium at intermission and threw up in a jade bush behind the theater.

After that first performance, however, the play improved steadily. By the end of the run, I felt that the production was exciting although still somewhat unwieldy. Nonetheless, when the play closed, I felt that the text should be rethought and reworked before I tried for another production.

Two years passed before I could actually look seriously at the play again. In 1988 I sat in a room at the Mayflower Hotel with an extraordinary director, Norman Renee. Norman suggested that I refocus the play and get rid of all the extraneous characters. "What extraneous characters," I asked? Norman told me to lose the gay uncle who stole all the jewels, to throw out Hank's stepson who doesn't bathe, and to highlight the mother and daughter story—even if it meant putting two bathrooms on stage! I wondered how my agent would react.

I went to work revising the play. I cut Uncle Bundy and the jewel plot completely; I transformed Willhite (Hank's stepson) into Brighton, Teddy's rich cousin; and I focused on the mother and daughter relationship without adding another bathroom to the set.

We performed the revised version at the Manhattan Theater Club Second Stage in the spring of 1988. Critics were kept out and the hope was that after working out the kinks in the smaller stage, we would transfer to the main stage in the fall. That did not happen. Although I found the production electrifying and provocative, the producer felt it was far too extreme, even embarrassing. I argued that I wanted the play to be extreme, I wanted it to be RED—the color of passion and shame—not pink or rose or fuchsia.

The Debutante Ball was banned from the Manhattan Theater Club main stage and has never been reviewed in New York City. It has, however, been produced in various theaters around the world, always to mixed response. It was a stunning failure in London, a smash hit in Hamburg. I'm not sure what that says about the play, or, in fact, about the Germans; but I do know that *The Debutante Ball* will always be dear to my heart because that's where it comes from. Although I have altered the cut of the gown, I have never changed its color. It is still red.

THE CHARACTERS

JEN DUGAN PARKER TURNER   the debutante's mother

TEDDY PARKER   the debutante

VIOLET MOONE   the maid

HANK TURNER   Teddy's stepfather, Jen's second husband,
  a wealthy attorney

BLISS WHITE   Teddy's half-sister, Jen's older daughter

BRIGHTON PARKER   Teddy's cousin, Jen's nephew

FRANCES WALKER   Hank's deaf niece

THE SETTING

The setting of the entire play is the upstairs parlor and connecting bathroom in the Turner mansion located in Hattiesburg, Mississippi, a small Southern town. Both rooms should be designed with stunning opulent elegance. The occupants have only recently moved into the mansion; therefore, there is still a sense of perfection and polish, nothing has begun to tarnish.

There are six entrances and exits leading to the parlor. On stage left, there is an entrance that leads to the outer hallway and the main staircase; and there is a staircase leading up to the third story. Upstage there is an entrance that leads to the back stairway and on down into the kitchen; and there is also a balcony with a stone railing. Stage right there is a door leading to Jen's bedroom and a door leading to the bathroom. There is also a connecting door between Jen's bedroom and the bath; thus there are two entrances and exits to the bathroom.

The bathroom should be magnificent with a crystal chandelier, marble floors, gold faucets, and a dressing table. There is a toilet located far stage right in an alcove.

TIME   Autumn.

Act I

SCENE ONE

In the bathroom, VIOLET MOONE, *a black woman in a maid's uniform, is scrubbing the bathroom mirror. She pauses a moment, then begins making noises like a bird.*

VIOLET Caw, caw, ahya. Caw, caw.

In the living room, JEN PARKER TURNER, *a lovely, lithe woman with black flickering eyes, begins giving instructions to her daughter,* TEDDY PARKER, *who stands in the wings of the balcony dressed in her white debutante's gown.* TEDDY *is a thin and strange looking girl with large, frightened eyes and tight, colorless lips.*

JEN And now, announcing Miss Theadora Jenniquade Parker Turner. (TEDDY *slowly and stiffly moves to the center of the balcony. Throughout the following,* TEDDY *attempts to follow* JEN's *instructions*)

Now turn majestically towards the audience, filling the room with your stunningly youthful presence. Remember your eye contact. Keep the chin up. Now let's see an elegant shimmer of a smile. Yes! Oh Yes! Now for your grand bow.

(JEN *demonstrates for* TEDDY)

Remember your grand bow must be full, radiant, magnificent! You are one hundred times more beautiful and alive than any of the jackasses sitting out in that banquet hall. You're a goddess and they're all swine. Do you have that?

TEDDY Yes, ma'am.

JEN Fine. Now bow to the swine. Oh, wonderful, Teddy. Flawlessly done. Now for the ascension. Keeping the neck long, chin up. Eyes rising over the swine. Shimmering smile. Glorious. Now turn around, slowly, I want to see the whole gown. Oh, now isn't that magnificent. The cut of the back is simply divine. Don't you feel divine?

TEDDY Divine. I feel divine.

JEN Oh yes, and once you have on your jeweled cape and the diamond tiara—Oh, and of course, your corrective makeup.

TEDDY Right, the corrective makeup. That'll help, won't it?

JEN Goodness, yes. Lord knows we'd all be hideous without it. I know, I'll run down and get your cape. You go into my bathroom and fix your face with the new 'round-the-clock makeup kit. That way we'll be able to get a better sense of the ensemble as a whole.

TEDDY Alright, Sweet Mama, I'll go fix it.

JEN Good.

> (JEN *exits down the back stairs*)

TEDDY I'll go fix my face. My face. Face.

> (*In the bathroom* VIOLET *is scrubbing the floor. Once again she makes sounds like a bird*)

VIOLET Caw, caw, ahya, ahya. Caw, caw, caw.

> (TEDDY *bursts into the bathroom*)

Oh, you scared me.

TEDDY Who are you?

VIOLET Violet Moone. I'm working here . . . for today.

TEDDY Why were you making those strange sounds?

VIOLET I don't know. I's just thinking 'bout the time when I heard them birds.

TEDDY What birds?

VIOLET Well, first I thought it was some wild child crying. So I went outside in the pouring rain t'hunt for it and then flapping up outta the trees I saw all them colors flying. The most beautiful colors alive— just coming up outta them trees in the drowning rain. All them lost birds shrieking this wild, mournful cry like there ain't nothing left but dying. My mama come and tol' me that them was tropical parrot birds and they liked t'mimic the talk they hear. It always stuck with me wondering, 'bout where they would of heard such mournful crying t'recollect.

TEDDY A lot of people cry. They could of heard it . . . anywhere.

VIOLET Well, I come t'figure it musta been somewhere on the long journey that took them birds away from the warm, sunny climate they was so lonesomely homesick for. Ya see 'cause a bird's a sign.

TEDDY What sorta sign?

VIOLET A sign a' change. And that's why I'm going off to—sunny, tropical L.A., California. They got real sand there, and fruit trees and a big, big ocean a'water.

TEDDY Umm. Well, maybe that's where I'll send my baby off to.

VIOLET You got a baby?

TEDDY (*Pointing to her stomach*) Yeah. In here.

VIOLET Oh.

TEDDY Violet, would you please hand me the Band-Aid box from up there?

VIOLET (*Handing her the box*) Here.

TEDDY Thank you.

> (TEDDY *opens the Band-Aid box, takes out a cigarette and match-book*)

Wanna smoke?

> (VIOLET *shakes her head.* TEDDY *lights up*)

Me, I love to smoke.

> (BLISS WHITE *and* HANK TURNER *enter from the main stairs carrying an enormous amount of baggage: a tattered suitcase; a beat-up trunk; a box with a badminton racket, board game, small, artificial Christmas tree tied to it with rope, a bird cage, etc.* BLISS *has white skin and mauve lips. She carries a huge stuffed animal. She is slender; her silky clothes seem to stick to her skin.* HANK *is a big lumbering man. He looks uncomfortable in his expensive business suit*)

HANK I'm not sure where Jen got off to.

BLISS Oh, oh, oh. Gracious God! Another stunning room!

HANK Well, the third story still needs a lot of work, but Jen wanted us all moved in here for Teddy's debutante deal.

> (*In the bathroom,* TEDDY *smokes her cigarette as she mercilessly plucks her eyebrows with a pair of tweezers*)

TEDDY I don't like hair. I abhor it.

BLISS And where is our prominent Hattiesburg Debutante? Why, she must be on pins and needles.

HANK She was, ah, down modeling her gown for us earlier this morning—

> (JEN *enters from the back stairway. She carries* TEDDY'S *satin cape*)

Jen, honey, hello—

BLISS Oh, Mama, Mama! Sweet, Sweet Mama!

JEN Bliss, you've arrived! My darling child.

BLISS Oh, Mama, it's been so long. I've missed you so much!

JEN Well, it's wonderful of you to come up from New Orleans for your sister's debut. I just hope you can—stay the weekend.

BLISS Of course. I—of course. Delightful.

JEN I've told Hank all about you. Isn't it true, we don't look a thing alike?

HANK Well, you're both mighty good-looking to me.

BLISS Oh, isn't he the charmer. Why, he'll just turn me giddy as a goose.

HANK (*After a beat*) So, Jen, how's Frances? Did she get in all right?

JEN I don't know.

HANK Didn't you pick her up?

JEN Was I supposed to?

HANK Good Lord, we discussed it thirty minutes last night!

JEN Oh, now I remember. She was going to have pansies pinned to her lapel.

HANK (*Looking at his watch*) God, the poor girl was due in at the Trailway Station over an hour and a half ago. Christ on a crutch! What's she gonna do?! She can't call anyone! She can't talk!

JEN I feel dreadful about this.

HANK Well, I've got to get right over there and try to locate the girl. I just hope to hell I find her! Holy God and dog shit, don't let her be lost!

(HANK *exits down the front stairway*)

JEN Poor Hank. He flares up like that since he stopped smoking.

(JEN *takes a compact case out of her pocket, opens it and takes out a cigarette*)

BLISS Yes, I can tell he's really a dear. Just a dear. Oh, Mama, you're smoking again.

JEN Yes, damnit. Don't tell Teddy.

BLISS Oh, I won't. I wouldn't. I won't.

(VIOLET *enters from the bathroom. She carries a pail*)

JEN Oh, Violet, go down front and start waxing the entrance hall. When you finish that, wash all the front windows, then start ironing the linen and stuffing the shrimp.

(VIOLET *exits down the front stairs, making noises like a bird*)
Oh, the shrimp! I'm boiling butterfly shrimp! They've probably completely disintegrated. Bliss, you run this cape in to Teddy. She's down there in that bathroom.

BLISS So, Mama, where shall I stay?

JEN Oh, anywhere up on the third floor. I believe there's a bed up there somewhere.

(JEN *exits down the back stairway.*

BLISS *looks at the cape with envy.*

In the bathroom TEDDY *takes the tweezers and violently scratches her face*)

TEDDY My Lord. My Lord. My face. My face.

(BLISS *heads toward the bathroom*)

BLISS Teddy! Teddy! Teddy Bear!

TEDDY Bliss? Is that you?

(BLISS *enters* JEN's *bathroom*)

BLISS Oh, Teddy, there you are, honey! Give me a hug! I want a hug.

TEDDY Oh, Bliss! Bliss!

BLISS Lord in heaven, what a luxurious bathroom.

TEDDY How are you?

BLISS (*Pulling back and looking at* TEDDY) Good Christ, what's that on your face?

TEDDY A scratch. A cat scratched me. It was beige colored.

BLISS My God. Well, don't worry, we'll find something in here to fix it up with.

(*Looking through her bag*)

Hmm. But first let me put on just a dash of mascara. I see people so much better when I'm wearing mascara. Oh God!

TEDDY What?

BLISS You're smoking again?

TEDDY Don't tell Mama. Swear you won't tell Mama.

BLISS Oh, I won't. I wouldn't. I won't.

(TEDDY *is dubious*)

So how is Mama anyway? Do you think she still hates me for being born?

(TEDDY *shrugs.* BLISS *begins putting makeup on herself*)

It's so unfair. And now I'm forced to plead with her to take me in.

TEDDY You mean to live here?

BLISS I have no choice. I'm destitute, penniless, deserted and alone. No one wants me. No one can stand me.

TEDDY What happened to your dog trainer boyfriend?

BLISS Oh, he said I couldn't dance. It's not true. I can dance. I dance. You've seen me dance!

TEDDY Uh huh.

BLISS In an unprovoked rage, he threw all of my belongings out of the window. I had to scrape this blush up off the sidewalk and put it in a plastic bag. The few fine things from my marriage to the fat man were lost or destroyed.

(*She sighs and begins putting makeup on* TEDDY)

11 SCENE ONE

So anyway, how is my former husband doing? Is Tommy still repulsively overweight?

TEDDY He's awfully large.

BLISS And how's my baby, Butterball?

TEDDY She's getting bigger and bigger.

BLISS God, I'm sick with guilt I never send Butterball anything at all. And I do love her so. She's my one child. It's just I hate to think about her.

> (about TEDDY's *makeup*)

There, that looks much better.

TEDDY Tell me, Bliss, boys and men, they know, don't they? I mean they know a girl's eyelids aren't really colored bright green and her lips aren't really so dark and red and shiny. They know that, don't they?

BLISS Of course they're aware it's something of an illusion.

TEDDY Then why do they like it? Why do they want it? It's all a big trick.

BLISS Well, uh, my, Teddy . . .

> (*The doorbell rings*)

BLISS Ah, chimes! Chimes! I love the chimes! I wonder who's coming? I wonder who's there? Oh, who could it be?

> (TEDDY *takes off her debutante gown*)

TEDDY Brighton's coming over. He's taking me to the hair salon.

BLISS Brighton is coming *here*? He's actually speaking to Mama?

> (TEDDY *puts on a black raincoat. She pulls the hood up over her head*)

TEDDY They all speak to her now that I'm having my debut.

BLISS You mean Mama is back in Theadora Parker's good graces?

TEDDY Yes, she is. Everyone has high hopes about my entrance into society. It's gonna turn everything around for us. I look divine in my gown.

BLISS Divine. I'm sure. Divine.

(BRIGHTON PARKER *enters from the front stairway with* VIOLET *leading him.* BRIGHTON *is a very well-dressed, proper young man. He wears horn-rimmed glasses and carries a cane*)

VIOLET She's up here someplace.

BRIGHTON (*About the room*) Utterly atrocious. Ghastly. Hideous. Unspeakable.

(*To Violet*)

I know you. Your mother, Candy Moone, used to work for my grandmother, Theadora.

VIOLET Yeah, I remember that lady. She rode in a wheelchair and fixed my mama leftover luncheon meat sandwiches to go.

BRIGHTON Yes, Grandmother's very generous. She's always thinking of others.

(TEDDY *puts a pair of wool socks on her hands*)

BLISS Teddy, why are you wearing socks on your hands?

TEDDY I wear them now instead of mittens.

BLISS Oh, thank God for my pharmaceutical regimen.

(BLISS *takes a pill.* TEDDY *enters the parlor from the bathroom*)

BRIGHTON Teddy, must you always wear that black raincoat?

TEDDY You never know about the weather.

(BLISS *enters from the bathroom*)

BLISS Brighton! Brighton! It's me! I'm home. I've returned!

BRIGHTON Yes, I see. So you have.

BLISS Gracious Lord, merciful heavens, that's Daddy's dog head cane you're carrying. What in the world possesses you to fraternize with that grotesque piece of memorabilia?

BRIGHTON Grandmother gave it to me after Uncle Theodore died. I carry it with me as a reminder.

BLISS A reminder of gruesomeness.

BRIGHTON Teddy, we don't have much time.

TEDDY I'm all ready. I'm all fine.

BLISS But first, won't y'all and the maid please help me carry up my luggage?

BRIGHTON All of this is yours?

BLISS I couldn't decide what to wear. So, Brighton, can you believe it? Mama's happily rich all over again.

> (TEDDY, VIOLET, BRIGHTON *and* BLISS *start hauling luggage up the stairs*)

BRIGHTON It is amazing. I never thought she'd marry that professional boor, even for the sake of money.

BLISS Why, I hear Hank Turner's very brilliant. They say he can talk spun gold in a courtroom.

BRIGHTON Yes, well, he did manage to save Aunt Jen's neck. And that was certainly quite a feat.

TEDDY No talking, no talking, no talking about any trials. That's all over. That's all behind us.

BRIGHTON (*To* TEDDY) Where're you going?

TEDDY I like to wait down in the car. That big black car.

> (TEDDY *exits down the main stairway*)

BRIGHTON She's upset. She's got problems.

VIOLET I know 'bout one of 'em.

(They exit up the stairs. JEN comes up the back stairs carrying a beautiful bouquet of debutante roses)

JEN Teddy! Where are you, my darling child? My wondrous salvation? Your debutante bouquet has arrived.

(JEN enters the bathroom)

Teddy?

(JEN sees TEDDY is not there. She twirls around smelling the bouquet)

They're so beautiful. Like all the untold secrets of the angels.

(JEN looks at herself in the mirror, smiling sweetly. Her smile disappears)

Ah. Hmm, why'd you have to get to be such an old bag of bones?

(VIOLET and BRIGHTON come walking down the stairs)

BRIGHTON It's amazing. The higher you go, the worse it gets. I'd rather live on a bed of nails than spend one night in this teratogeny.

VIOLET It's kinda scary.

JEN *(exits from bathroom)* Brighton! To see your face again.

BRIGHTON Aunt Jen, hello.

JEN Well, come here and kiss me, my cherished child.

BRIGHTON I, no. No thank you.

JEN Please. What's wrong? You always said I was your favorite aunt.

BRIGHTON Yes, and Uncle Theodore was Grandmother's only son.

JEN How pompous you've become clutching that silly cane. Oh well, we'll turn it all around. Here, just look at Teddy's debutante bouquet. Don't the roses remind you of the untold secrets of angels.

BRIGHTON Yes, but angels don't keep secrets.

JEN No, then where's Teddy? I want her to see it.

BRIGHTON I believe she's down in Grandmother's limousine.

(*JEN runs out on the balcony and waves below to TEDDY*)

JEN Teddy! Oh, Teddy!

BRIGHTON God, who'd ever think it? Her with those frail white hands and flowered charm. Who'd ever believe?

VIOLET What?

JEN (*Disappears on the balcony*) Look up here, child!

BRIGHTON That she murdered her own husband in that violent fashion.

JEN (*offstage*) Your bouquet, my angel!

VIOLET Oh, Lordy! Is she the one from in the newspapers?

BRIGHTON That's she.

VIOLET And the girl in the white dress, was it her daddy was murdered?

BRIGHTON (*Nods yes*) Yes. My Uncle Theodore. Three years ago.

VIOLET Got bludgeoned to death with a cast-iron skillet.

JEN (*offstage*) Tonight's going to be all you ever dreamed! I promise you! I promise!

(*Lights fade to blackout*)

SCENE TWO

BLISS *is standing with one leg in* JEN's *bathroom sink. She shaves her leg in a tattered peach teddy as she sings an upbeat Spanish song.*

JEN *sits at her dressing table in a beautiful rose-colored slip. She is putting ointment onto sores on her skin.*

JEN (*Laughing with delight*) Oh, how sweet it is! How divine!

BLISS Marvelous, Mommie! Marvelous!

JEN Just think, Bliss, tonight I'm going to get them all back—

BLISS Resplendent revenge!

JEN (*Running on*) Everyone in this town who ever shunned or ostracized us.

BLISS Let them eat words! Oh, let them eat words.

(JEN *puts on a robe*)

JEN Imagine. We'll all drive out to the ball—together again! Theadora Parker's going to enter my new house and shake my dirty hand which will be dripping with jewels and gold.

BLISS Dear old Grandmama.

JEN Ha! After my trial, the heartless bitch was happy to see all we had auctioned off to the highest bidder.

BLISS Yes, she was very bitter about it all. Very bitter.

JEN She's hoping tonight will give some new air of respectability to the memory of her infamous son. To the memory of her son. Why, this has got nothing to do with that wretched man.

BLISS You never loved Daddy, did you, Mama? Even on your wedding day?

JEN Of course not, Bliss. I told you that.

BLISS I'm glad you're with Hank now.

JEN Yes, well, I never get tired of marrying for money.

BLISS No, why should you?

JEN Exactly. Teddy needs every advantage. She's been put on probation up at Ole Miss. The tri-Delts have threatened to expel her—for idiosyncratic behavior.

BLISS Well, frankly, her social skills do need a good deal of refining. She went out today wearing socks on her hands instead of mittens. She's just trying to get attention. It's repulsive. She's smoking again, too.

JEN No! Oh, Goddammit! The little liar! What am I going to do?

BLISS (*Shaving under her arm*) You've done all you can. You've married Hank. You have this splendid mansion for her to live in. Why, tonight she's going to be presented at the Hattiesburg Debutante Ball in a Paris gown strewn with antique pearls. It really oughta be enough for anyone.

>   (*Cutting herself with the razor*)

Aaah! Damnation! I cut myself. Look at this gash.

JEN (*Really sick*) No, I can't. I swear. Really, I used to could look at bloody things, now they get me so sick.

BLISS It's all right. I'll soak it up. It's not so bad.

(BLISS *soaks up the blood.*

JEN *leaves the bathroom and goes into the main room.*

HANK *comes up the main stairway. He is dripping with sweat*)

HANK She's nowhere to be found! I've had to notify the police. They're all out searching for her. An Officer Shackelford is waiting downstairs to keep us posted.

(BLISS *enters the living room in her teddy*)

BLISS (*Showing her underarm*) Look, Mama, the bleeding has spontaneously subsided.

(HANK *paces over by the phone*)

HANK God, I just don't know what to do. I can't call up my dying sister and tell her I've lost her only child. Oh, what have I done?! What have I done?!

(HANK *goes to pour himself a straight bourbon*)

JEN Oh, Hank, please, don't start drinking now. Remember tonight's Teddy's Debutante Ball.

HANK Screw the ball, woman! I've lost my deaf niece!

(VIOLET *comes up the back stairs with a huge tray of unpolished silver, silver polish and rags.* VIOLET *is uneasy in* JEN'S *presence*)

JEN Oh, Violet, thank goodness. You've brought up the silver.

VIOLET It's all right here—every piece of it.

BLISS My rings! I haven't got on my rings! I'm flushed all over with embarrassment. I'm simply deshabe without them.

JEN The flowers! The flowers! Have they arrived?

VIOLET Yeah. Big bunches of 'em.

(BLISS *flees into* JEN'S *bathroom to retrieve her rings*)

JEN (*To* VIOLET) Bring the red ones up here. The white ones stay below.

VIOLET That's where I'll keep 'em.

(VIOLET *exits down the back stairs.* HANK *pours himself another drink*)

HANK God Almighty. God Almighty.

JEN Hank, please, I know you're upset—

HANK Yes, Jen, I am upset. Very upset.

(BLISS *enters the main room, spraying herself with perfume*)

BLISS I'm drenching myself in lilac perfume. That's all there is to do.

HANK My sister, Sue, is literally eaten up with cancer—

BLISS (*Still spraying*) Ugh.

HANK She could drop dead any minute—

BLISS (*Still spraying*) Poor thing.

HANK She sends her only daughter down here to go to this goddamn ball in a last-ditch effort to find a husband—

BLISS (*Still spraying*) How pathetic!

HANK And what do we do? We lose the girl! She's gone. She's lost. She wasn't picked up.

JEN Please, she's not lost. She's misplaced. Frances will be retrieved. It's inevitable.

HANK It'd suit you just fine if she never showed up. You didn't want my family included. Admit it, Jen. You never did.

JEN We're all delighted to have Frances.

HANK You're not delighted, Jen. You never even found her a date. You didn't mail out her invitation. You're convinced she won't fit in. Come on! Face it! Look at the evidence!

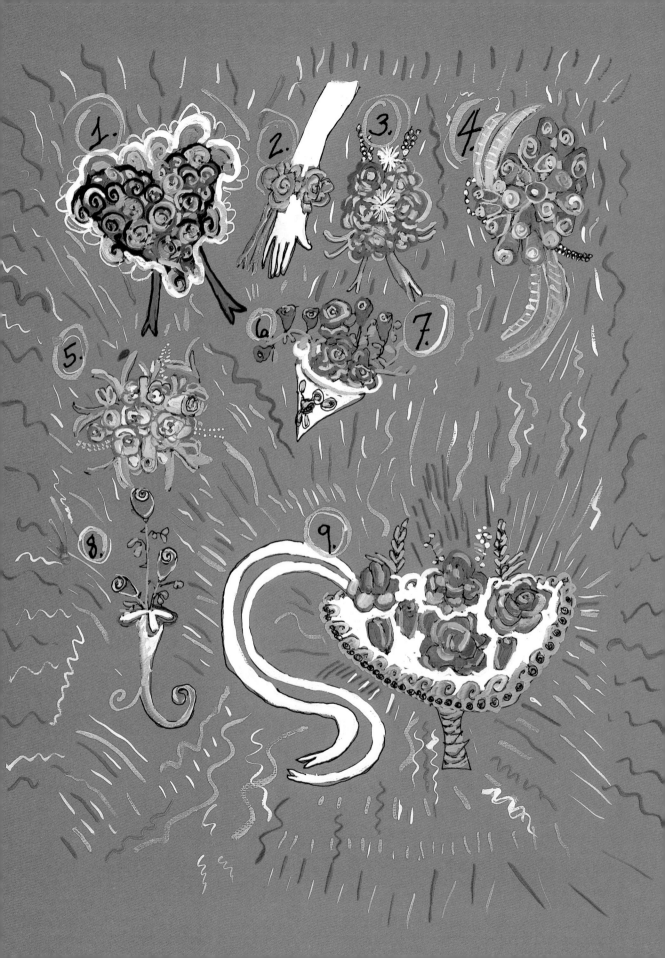

JEN She will fit in. We'll fit her in! Now please, Hank, stop raving like a lunatic—go out on the balcony and have a cigarette.

HANK I don't smoke anymore!

JEN Yes, you do. You do.

(JEN *takes a cigarette and lighter out of her robe pocket, lights the cigarette and hands it to* HANK)

There you are. There's your smoke.

HANK Alright, Jen. Alright.

(HANK *goes out on the balcony to smoke his cigarette*)

BLISS Men. They're all wild. They're all crazy.

JEN I know how to handle him. I can run him. It's just sometimes I don't have the patience. There's only so much I can bear to swallow.

BLISS Absolutely. I don't know why his niece had to be invited. She's spent her whole life on some dirt poor farm. She's probably never been to an occasion of any sort. I'm sure she can't dance; she can't hear; she can't make chit-chat.

(VIOLET *enters up the back stairway with an armload of red flowers*)

VIOLET Here're the red ones. The white ones are staying below.

BLISS (*Swooning*) Oh, how lovely! How divine! Mama, I must have a corsage for tonight. I need money for an enormous arrangement. I want to erupt with foliage.

(JEN *starts arranging the flowers*)

JEN Yes, you expect to be given everything your heart desires. You'll just lap it right up off a silver platter. Why, my father never even once gave me a gift or a remembrance of any kind.

BLISS Yes, you told me.

JEN At Christmas time I'd invent pets he'd given me, like a pony or a puppy or a parakeet.

BLISS I remember you named your pony Dodie.

JEN Later I'd tell all my friends and acquaintances the pet had died. That way I was able to save face. That's how I did it.

BLISS Yes, I know all that, Mama.

JEN Well, then, polish the silver! Do something useful! Life isn't just some parade passing by!

(BLISS *starts polishing the silver*)

Violet, bring up the party favors. I want to arrange them in this urn. That way they'll be a surprise. No one will know what they're picking. No one will see what's coming.

VIOLET Caw, caw, ahya!

(VIOLET *exits down the back stairway*)

JEN Christ, I'd love to fire her. Unfortunately, I can't. I fired all the help yesterday. Do you know she's the only person in the whole town Hank could find who'd come in and work for me today. What am I, a leper?

(TEDDY *and* BRIGHTON *come up the main stairway.* TEDDY *wears a black raincoat with the hood pulled up over her head and socks on her hands*)

TEDDY (*Breathlessly*) Listen, everyone, there's a policeman downstairs. He's smoking a cigar in the front hallway. What's he want? Mama, who's he come for?

BLISS Oh, he's only here about that deformed, I mean, deaf girl, Hank's niece. She's still lost.

TEDDY Oh, well, I hope they find her.

J E N Don't worry. We're going to find Frances. Everything will work out perfectly. It always does. Now, Teddy, what time is your friend David Brickman arriving from Atlanta?

T E D D Y Oh. Oh, him. Him. This is very upsetting.

J E N What?

T E D D Y He's not coming.

J E N What do you mean he's not coming? This has been arranged for months. His name's in the program. He's your official escort.

T E D D Y I know, I know. It's dreadful. But his mother called up and said he fell down out on his lawn and broke his limb in two.

J E N He what?

T E D D Y His left limb just broke in two.

J E N But this can't be.

> (T E D D Y *sniffs, then quickly pulls off her hood to show her hair which has been put up on her head in a bouffant style.*
>
> V I O L E T *comes up the back stairway with a basket of party favors*)

T E D D Y How do you like my hair? They did a nice job. Don't you see how the hairpiece adds a lot of fullness to the head.

B R I G H T O N It's very attractive.

B L I S S (*Overlapping from "like my hair"*) Well, they certainly poofed it out.

V I O L E T (*Overlapping from "nice job"*) Real fancy.

J E N Give me his number, Teddy. I'm calling his parents. This is an outrage. You tell me this boy is from one of the finest families in Atlanta and he does this!

T E D D Y Please, Mama, he didn't mean to take the spill.

JEN I'll spill him! He can't back out on us at the last minute. Get me his number, Teddy. Goddamnit, the little bastard's not gonna ditch us like dirt. Now run get me his number!

TEDDY Yes, Mama. I'll go get the number. I'll go get it.

(TEDDY *runs down the hall to her bedroom*)

JEN I won't be stepped on anymore. No one is ruining this night! No one!

BLISS Please, it's alright, Mama. Don't get upset. Whatever you do—just don't—do it.

JEN (*To* BLISS) Did you clean up all of that hair in my bathroom sink?

BLISS I think so.

JEN Well, make sure! You know how I hate hair! I abhor it! I can't stand to look at it. It makes my skin crawl. Now, go and check on that hair.

BLISS It's always the *same* whenever I come home. It's always the *same.*

(BLISS *runs into the bathroom and lights up a cigarette*)

JEN Violet, go brew some tea. We need tea!

(VIOLET *exits down the back stairway*)

JEN (*To* BRIGHTON) Why are you looking at me like that?

BRIGHTON It's so bewildering to me how I ever could have believed in your foolish charm.

JEN You were a lonely, fanciful child. We made each other laugh. I used to let you bake buttermilk biscuits. You'd always eat a ball of the dough.

BRIGHTON Yes, I enjoyed eating that ball of dough. I found it tasty. I believe I actually preferred it to the biscuits.

(TEDDY *enters*)

TEDDY Here, Sweet Mama. Here's the number.

JEN Thank you.

(JEN *goes to the phone*)

BRIGHTON (*To* TEDDY) Why can't anything ever work out with you people?

TEDDY We're snake bit.

JEN Teddy, the telephone number you've given me is missing a digit.

TEDDY Let me see. I thought it was correct. It's the one he gave me. Oh no, I must have deleted a digit.

JEN Goddamnit, I'm all set to bless them straight to hell. Call information! We need directory assistance!!!

(TEDDY *goes to call on the phone*)

BRIGHTON Really, Aunt Jen, if the boy's leg is broken, I can't understand what good it's going to do to make a scene.

JEN That young man is going to honor his commitment to Teddy. He's obligated to us. He'll have to send a replacement.

TEDDY They're unlisted. They're so rich and powerful they're not even listed.

JEN Please, Teddy, don't worry. We'll fix it. I'm sure Brighton knows some marvelous young men.

BRIGHTON Me? You can't expect me! Good Lord, this is the very day of the ball. All of my affiliates have made arrangements months in advance.

TEDDY They're all booked up.

JEN Oh, come on, Brighton, anyone will do. A young boy. A grandfather type. We're not being particular at the moment. Think! Think!

BRIGHTON Let me think. Let me think! Let me think!! No, I can't think! I can't think! There's no one.

TEDDY No one.

BRIGHTON No one at all.

JEN Well, then you'll just have to take her yourself.

BRIGHTON That's impossible. As the official representative from the Parker family, I'm presenting her at the ball. The escort has got to be different from the presenter.

JEN Oh, you're right. God. Good God.

TEDDY Please, Sweet Mama. Don't despair. I have a good solution.

JEN What?

TEDDY I'll send regrets. I'll say I have an acid stomach.

BRIGHTON I suppose if things can't be done properly. I mean, the whole purpose of tonight was to enhance the Parker family image, not to disgrace it further.

JEN (*Overlapping*) Shut up! You're not talking anymore. Shut up! Shut up! Let me think. Let me think. Hank! You'll go with Hank. That's all. It's a radical move, but he's all we've got. Hank!

TEDDY Mama, wait—

JEN (*Calling out on the balcony*) Hank, dear, are you about!

BRIGHTON You'll make us all laughingstocks.

(HANK *enters from the balcony*)

HANK Yes, Jen, what is it?

JEN Hank, dear, we've run into a little snag. Teddy requires an escort for this evening's ball. And she's hoping you'll comply.

HANK You want me to be her date?

JEN (*To* TEDDY) See, dear, he'd be delighted.

BRIGHTON This is ridiculous. The escort is supposed to be a young, eligible man, not some ancient old goat who's married to the debutante's mother.

TEDDY (*In a whisper*) Unfortunately, I don't think he can waltz. I observed him at your wedding and he couldn't waltz.

JEN Nonsense. Hank has a natural grace. Here, take her in your arms. Spin her around the ballroom floor.

    (TEDDY *and* HANK *awkwardly begin to waltz*)

See there. There's nothing to it. Try to breathe. Breathe. Keep breathing.

    (HANK *steps on* TEDDY's *foot*)

TEDDY Ah, my toes! He stepped on my toes! I think they're all broken for good!

HANK I'm so sorry. I'm such an ox. I'm known for my clumsiness.

JEN Teddy, please, Hank would never break your toes. We'll rehearse his waltzing. It won't be a problem.

BRIGHTON She doesn't want to go with him. It's apparent. I think we all know why.

TEDDY Oh, please, Sweet Mama, I just don't think I can go. My toes are broken.

JEN Listen to me, Teddy. I wish we could find you the perfect escort. I've tried so hard to make this night just what you wanted. Why do you think I've spent this last year planning and preparing and coordinating

everything especially for you. Why, I had the florist make up nine different rose bouquets before I approved the one that was exactly exquisitely right for your ensemble. I know I can never change the past. But please, please don't deny me this ferocious dream I have of giving you a future.

TEDDY Yes. I'll go with him. He'll be my date.

JEN Fine, glorious.

HANK I don't like twisting her arm.

BRIGHTON She despises the man.

TEDDY I'll need a lot of makeup, though. A lot of it. All over my face.

JEN We'll dance all night. It will be a spectacular occasion. We'll always remember it.

(*VIOLET enters from the main stairway with a tea tray*)

VIOLET The deaf girl. She's come. She's down there. She's gotten all dusty!

(*Everyone heads out the front hall doorway*)

HANK Frances. Thank God! She's alive! Thank God. My dear, Frances.

JEN (*Overlapping*) See there! I knew it would all work out perfectly!

BRIGHTON (*Overlapping*) It's unbelievable! Now the deaf girl comes! Tonight will be so mortifying.

TEDDY (*Relishing the idea*) I wonder what it's like for her when she can't even hear anything at all? Nothing at all.

(*They all exit. BLISS sits alone in JEN's bathroom. She powders herself with an enormous powder puff.*

FRANCES WALKER enters the parlor from the back stairway. She is tall and strong and wears a dust-covered suit. She moves

*awkwardly around the room carrying her dust-laden suitcase
and shoes.*

BLISS *moves from the bathroom into the main room to get
a drink to wash down some pills she is taking.* BLISS *spots*
FRANCES)

BLISS Oh, hello.

(FRANCES *has had three summers of training at a deaf school;
so she knows some sign language and can read lips somewhat.
However, since almost no one around her knows sign language,
she has invented her own way of communicating—a very unique
pantomime along with attempts at speaking words. This will
have to be developed by the actress*)

Well, how do you do? I'm Bliss White.

FRANCES "HELLO, I'M FRANCES WALKER."

BLISS Pardon? What's that? Oh! Oh, my God! You're the cousin.

(BLISS *takes a pill; yelling and enunciating*)

Yes, so won-der-ful to meet you. I'm *Bliss* White. Comprende vous,
ma chere?

(FRANCES *nods yes and no*)

Yes, Bliss. Je m'appelle, Bliss.

FRANCES "BLISS."

BLISS Yes! Very good! Tres bien! Assezez vous gentilmente. While
I go get some help.

(FRANCES *shakes her head in utter despair. She can hardly re-
frain from crying*)

FRANCES "THIS HOUSE IS TOO BIG. TOO BEAUTI-
FUL."

BLISS (*Overlapping*) What's wrong? Why, you did very well.

FRANCES "WHY DID I EVER COME? WHAT A FOOL!"

BLISS Oh, I shouldn't have been speaking French.

FRANCES "MY MAMA'S SICK!"

BLISS (*Running on*) Why was I speaking Francais! Good gracious! Silly me.

FRANCES "I MUST GO. HOME. I GO. I GO."

BLISS Oh no, don't go. Stay here. Stay. Stay! Sit! Sit!

FRANCES "SIT. I'M NO DOG. I HATE DOGS."

BLISS Perhaps you'd like some tea.

FRANCES "WHEN I WALK, THIS DOG GROWLS AT ME AND BITES."

BLISS (*Overlapping*) Oh my! This is ghastly! Mama. Somebody. Help. Help me!

FRANCES "OH, I DON'T BELONG HERE. I'M ALL DIRTY."

BLISS Oh Lord. Oh Lordy.

FRANCES "LOOK AT THIS. I'M COVERED WITH FILTH."

BLISS (*Overlapping*) What? What? Oh dear, dear, dear.

FRANCES (*Overlapping*) "UGH, MY FEET. SMELL MY FEET."

BLISS Your feet?

FRANCES "OH, THEY STINK."

BLISS Stink? Your feet stink. Your feet stink!

FRANCES (*Overlapping*) "YEAH. YEAH. THEY DO!"

BLISS Oh, well, here, we'll just spray them with perfume. We'll drench them in perfume.

(BLISS *starts spraying* FRANCES' *feet with perfume*)

There. That's good. I'll make it right. You'll have fun. It will be a beautiful night for you. Your feet are lovely now. Just lovely.

(FRANCES *looks up at* BLISS *and smiles*)

FRANCES ''YOU ARE SO BEAUTIFUL.''

BLISS Yes. Well, anyway. Yes.

(BLISS *sprays herself with perfume.*)

(*Lights fade to blackout*)

SCENE THREE

It is evening. VIOLET *is wearing a formal maid's uniform. She is helping* HANK *finish dressing for the ball.* HANK *fidgets as* VIOLET *hooks him into his black cummerbund.* HANK *has a shred of toilet tissue stuck to his face over a cut he got shaving. Champagne has been laid out. The tea service has been cleared.*

HANK This waist thing's too tight. I feel like a stuck hog.

VIOLET That's as loose as it'll go.

HANK Damn! T'hell with all this debutante crap. It's turned Jen into a crazy woman. Why, it was no surprise to me when the maids and cook quit yesterday.

VIOLET (*Picking up his cuff links*) Here, I'll get on your studs.

HANK I just can't tell you, Violet, how much I appreciate your coming t'help us out here on such short notice. I wish you'd consider staying with us on a permanent basis.

VIOLET Well, thing is come Monday morning, me and my kids are headed out for L.A., California.

HANK I tell you, Violet, breaking into the entertainment world is not going to be nearly as simple as you may imagine. How would your mama have felt about you hauling all your kids off to a strange place like California?

VIOLET Well, I know, Mr. Turner, that at my age I've already been a jailbird and nobody expects much outta me. But I'll prove 'em wrong.

HANK I hope so, Violet, but I have some grave doubts about the practicality of your plans.

VIOLET Thing is ever since I was alive I've had this longing t'be a circus clown. Originally, I thought you had to be born a clown, and I cried all the time thinking how badly I felt 'cause I could never be turned from a black colored person into a funny clown person. Then one day watching TV, I discovered that clowns were man-made and if I just learned out at the circus school in California—I could change myself and become one, too. From then on, a whole wide life appeared up before me.

> (*Suddenly* JEN *appears at the top of the stairs in a glamorous satin emerald gown. She carries a dazzling gold jewelry case under her arm.* HANK *"oohs" at the sight of her*)

JEN Good evening, everyone! Oh, let's illuminate the sky! What a night! What a time! Oh, I'm so filled with excitement!

> (VIOLET *rushes out onto the balcony and starts lighting small lanterns*)

HANK God, your face.

JEN What?

HANK It sparkles.

JEN Oh, Hank. Hank! Hank!

HANK (*Overlapping*) Like a Christmas tree when you smile. Like a lit up Christmas tree.

JEN (*Laughing*) Yes, I feel aglow. I feel aglow.

HANK God, to hear you laugh. You know that first year we were married the only thing that ever made you smile even faintly was sitting and watching a rainstorm come in.

JEN Yes, you'd sit there with me and we'd watch the rain flood down.

HANK Later on you got to where you'd laugh just a little. Lord, it made me cry to hear you laugh so thin and strange. All I wanna do is be with you and hear your laughter soar.

JEN No, don't ever leave me.

> (TEDDY *enters from her room. She wears her debutante's gown, a white satin cape, silver slippers, and carries a glittering evening bag. She looks as though she is ready for battle*)

TEDDY Here I am, Mama! I'm ready for the ball!

JEN What a vision! Isn't she a vision!

HANK Oh my goodness, she's pretty.

JEN A belle! A real Southern belle.

TEDDY Clang, clang, clang.

JEN Here now, you must wear this diamond necklace. It's the perfect adornment to your gown.

> (JEN *takes a glittering necklace out of the jewel box*)

TEDDY Diamonds galore.

JEN Isn't it beautiful. Like a treasure from a cherub's tomb. Hank gave it to me for our anniversary.

HANK I love to give your mama things.

> (JEN *goes to put the necklace on* TEDDY)

HANK Remember the first gift I ever gave you?

JEN The Fiat?

HANK No, honey, you were still in jail and I brought you in that homegrown tomato.

JEN It's magnificent. How it sets off your eyes.

HANK You said it was the best tomato you'd ever had.

JEN Run look at your sweetself in the mirror. You're the purest angel. The dearest one.

> (TEDDY *goes into* JEN's *bathroom and stares at herself in the mirror*)

HANK You said each bite was like an endless summer. Don't you remember the tomato?

JEN Yes, of course, I'm very fond of vegetables.

> (*Holding up her jewels*)

Let me see, what should I wear? I want to appear enormously enriched! I want them all to be speechless with envy.

HANK God, you look so beautiful to me, I can't hardly stand it.

JEN Oh, butter me up some more. Please, butter me up some more.

> (VIOLET *enters from the balcony. All the outdoor lanterns have been lit*)

HANK (*To* VIOLET) Violet, come in here and look at her! Why, I'd like to eat her right up with a silver spoon. Mmm, mmm. Gobble, gobble.

JEN (*Uncomfortable*) Hank, please, butter me up, but don't fry me in fat.

HANK Sorry, I just can't help it.

> (HANK *knocks over a vase of flowers*)

JEN Oh, Hank, watch out! Those fresh flowers were sent in special for tonight!

HANK I'll get something t'sweep it up with.

(*The doorbell rings*)

JEN God, that's Teddy's grandmother. They're here.

(*To* HANK)

What's that toilet paper doing stuck on your face?

HANK (*Pulling it off*) Oh.

JEN Oh, Hank, would you run upstairs and lock my jewels back in the safe?

HANK Alright.

JEN Oh, and Hank, please don't come down without your jacket. Violet, would you get him his jacket?

(*To* HANK)

Now, Hank, I know how much fun it is for you to let everyone think you're just a loud, crazy, redneck who happens to have a brilliant mind; and if you want to hide behind that facade, well, that's up to you, because Teddy and I will be proud of you no matter what. And that's just the way we feel.

(JEN *exits down the main stairway.* HANK *turns to* VIOLET, *who is sweeping up the flowers*)

HANK Great. She's using reverse psychology on me. How brilliant. God, she's really changed since the day I met her in that little ol' county jail cell. I tell you one thing, Violet, a woman in distress is enormously attractive to a man. And if he thinks he's gonna be able to offer a bit of solace to her despair, well, he's a greased and cooked goose.

(HANK *exits up the staircase with the jewel box.* VIOLET *exits down the back stairway. In the bathroom,* TEDDY *puts roll-on deodorant behind her knees.*

FRANCES *slowly opens the bathroom door. She wears a home-made dress and holds a white fur stole lovingly in her arms)*

FRANCES *(Tentatively holding out the fur)* ''HI . . . COULD I . . . COULD I WEAR . . .''

TEDDY Have it. Have it. It's yours.

(FRANCES' face lights up. She throws the fur around her shoulders and spins around the room)

FRANCES ''OH, THANK YOU, TEDDY. THANK YOU! MANY WARM THANKS.''

(BLISS bursts into the bathroom wearing a green gown)

BLISS See there. I told you she'd let you wear it!

FRANCES ''IT'S THE SOFTEST THING I'VE EVER FELT IN MY LIFE.''

BLISS Yes, and it does make all the difference in the world! Oh, Teddy, Teddy. My God, if I were only in your slippers, this would be the most thrilling night of my life. Why, I could burst into hysterical tears thinking about how I was never ever allowed to be a debutante. Oh God, never to be allowed. Not allowed. The agony.

(TEDDY moans from her bowels)

Oh, good God, don't be such a silly. Things aren't that serious. Here, let's go out and have some pink champagne.

(They all move out into the parlor)

Come on now, we must be gay and frivolous tonight and spin ourselves into a high, high fever.

(FRANCES awkwardly imitates the way BLISS is spinning and gliding across the floor.

As she pours champagne)

That's it, Frances! Oh, what a stunning carriage! Doesn't she have the most stunning carriage!

TEDDY Oh, she does! Boy, she does. Clang! Clang! Clang!

(BLISS *hands out glasses of champagne*)

BLISS Here now, we must all drink up. It's a scientific fact that people who don't drink severely limit their spiritual development!

(*They all click glasses and dance about.* HANK *appears at the top of the stairs. He slides down the bannister. They all look up at him and gasp*)

HANK Good evening, ladies!

FRANCES ''UNCLE HANK!''

BLISS What an athletic performance! What an amazing feat!

HANK My, and don't the three of you look so pretty! Like three angels on a cake!

FRANCES (*Giving him a glass of champagne*) ''PUNCH!''

HANK Well, thank you, Frances. Cheers, everyone. Cheers.

BLISS I'm putting on some music! We must dance!

HANK (*To* TEDDY) Well, I have been practicing, if you'd like to give it a whirl, Miss Teddy.

(*The waltzing music begins*)

TEDDY Dancing's not for me.

HANK I'll look out for your toes.

TEDDY I'm saving myself for the ball.

(BLISS *waves a rose at* HANK *with a smile*)

BLISS I'll dance with you.

(BLISS *slings the rose over her shoulder*)

HANK Perhaps she's right. I am awful clumsy.

BLISS Oh, come on now. No fool, no fun.

(BLISS *and* HANK *start dancing awkwardly.* FRANCES *watches with awe*)

Ah, I love dancing. I've always dreamed of spending my life as a ballerina doll spinning madly on top of a jeweled music box.

(*Picking up a quarter that she spots*)

Oh, look, a quarter!

(*Pressing the coin into his palm*)

Here, you must keep it for me.

(*Turning to* TEDDY *and* FRANCES)

Look, everyone, isn't he marvelous! Why, he's just a natural!

(TEDDY *watches with interest as* FRANCES *applauds the couple.* JEN *and* BRIGHTON *enter from the main stairway*)

JEN Oh, very good! Why, Hank, your waltzing is looking so much better! Just don't let Bliss trip you up with her sense of rhythm. She's always been such an awkward dancer.

(BLISS *stops dancing and goes to the record player*)

HANK Jen, please don't treat the girl like that.

JEN Treat her like what? Teddy, Brighton's brought up your grandmother's tiara. Go put it on and then hurry downstairs.

(BRIGHTON *hands* TEDDY *the tiara.*

BLISS *scratches the needle across the record. There is a horrible screech.* BLISS *kicks the wall with her foot and bangs on it with her fist. Everyone looks at her*)

JEN Really, Bliss, please. I don't want to get into another tiff. I was just teasing you, silly.

BLISS Teasing me? That's teasing?

JEN Yes, because, you see, dancing is something that has always come so easily to me—

BLISS (*Swallowing pills with champagne*) Well, we all pale by comparison to you.

JEN Good then. You just keep on taking those pills, but they're going to kill you just like they killed Judy Garland. Only you won't have any fame, or money to show for it!

HANK Jen—

JEN (*To* HANK) And if you want to stay here and defend this pill-popper, please do! Everyone else, we're leaving right now!

(JEN *exits out the hall door.* BLISS *stops taking pills*)

HANK Sorry, honey. Sometimes I guess you'd just as soon she hit you with a stick.

BRIGHTON A stick perhaps, but not an iron skillet.

HANK Hey! You think that's funny?

BRIGHTON No, you're right. It's never funny when somebody gets away with murder.

(HANK *grabs* BRIGHTON's *tuxedo lapel*)

HANK You smug little bastard. You don't know shit.

BRIGHTON Maybe not. But ask Teddy. She knows the truth.

TEDDY (*To* BRIGHTON) I don't know anything. You're a liar. There's nothing that I know. Shut up. Just shut up! Oh, I need some more makeup. On my face. My face.

(TEDDY *goes to the bathroom where she proceeds to put on massive amounts of makeup*)

HANK (*To* BRIGHTON) After tonight I don't want you around here. I hope I'm making myself clear.

(HANK *exits down the main stairway*)

BRIGHTON You people! You people! You're all festering with secrets and lies. And that man! That man! Did you see how he walks? Just like a pig.

(BRIGHTON *laughs with a snort*)

BLISS Did you know, Brighton, that you snort when you laugh?

BRIGHTON No, I wasn't aware of it.

(*He laughs and snorts once more.*

BLISS *slings her champagne in his face*)

BLISS Then perhaps you'd better suppress your mirth.

(BRIGHTON *glares at her, too furious to move.* FRANCES *watches, amazed*)

BRIGHTON (*To* BLISS) Strange. Somehow, I always knew you were never really part of my family. Your mannerisms are different. They're affected and coarse. The older you get, the more apparent it becomes.

(BRIGHTON *turns and exits down the back stairway.*

TEDDY *comes out of the bathroom covered with makeup, wearing the tiara on her head. She holds and pushes up the skin on her face with her hands*)

TEDDY Oh, my face, the skin up on my face. They say it never stops growing. It just starts slowly sagging and slipping down. And soon, it'll kinda be hanging there like globs of meat on a bone.

(TEDDY *stops at the bar and takes a slug of bourbon from the bottle*)

BLISS You are so sophomoric, Teddy. Sometimes you are so goddamn sophomoric!

TEDDY (*Squirting breath spray*) I gotta go see my grandmother, Theadora. She's waiting down there for me. We're going off to the ball. But first I'd better remind her to hold that excess falling skin up on her face.

BLISS Go on down to your precious grandmother! I don't want any part of her or the rest of them! I'm glad my father was a fruit picker!!!

> (TEDDY *exits down the main stairway.*
>
> BLISS *turns to* FRANCES. *She mimes some of the following for* FRANCES)

Theodore wasn't my real father. Mama pretended he was, even though she was four months gone by the time they got married.

FRANCES ''A BABY?''

BLISS Yes. Me. I was the baby. My fruit picker father shot himself in the heart when he found out about her wedding.

FRANCES ''HURT HEART.''

BLISS Exactly. All of this came out at Mama's trial. My debut was cancelled. I married Tommy to escape; things went sour; I fled. Still there was a relief in knowing Theodore Parker bore me no relation. He was an abusive drug addict as well as an embezzler and thief. Even so, it's awful Mama—killed him. Ah, well, as you can see, it's all been very Byzantine.

> (BLISS *moves around the room. She feels sticky all over*)

God, these underpants are sticking to my skin. Here, let me get rid of them.

(BLISS *reaches up under her skirt and shimmies off her green silk underpants.* FRANCES *watches amazed*)

Sometimes I simply can't bear underwear. They're so nasty.

(FRANCES *suddenly reaches up under her dress and takes off her cotton panties and holds them up triumphantly.* BLISS *shakes her panties at* FRANCES. FRANCES *shakes hers at* BLISS.

Laughing, BLISS *runs with her panties to the balcony window and throws them over the edge.*)

Au revoir.

(FRANCES *holds her panties between her teeth and then slings them over the balcony railing.*

She looks back at BLISS *and shrugs.* BLISS *bursts into hysterical laughter.* FRANCES *starts laughing, too. They collapse together on the floor in heaps of laughter*)

Oh, God! Oh, God! I must go to the pot. Quick! Oh, God!

(BLISS *gets up and rushes into the bathroom.* FRANCES *rushes after her.* BLISS *hikes up her skirt as she dashes to the toilet in the alcove*)

Ah, what a relief! I have a teeny-tiny bladder. Everyone in our family does. That was the thing about being married to the fat man, all of his family had huge bladders. They could go solid months without peeing.

(BLISS *gets up, flushes the toilet and goes to put on more mascara.* FRANCES *is brushing on powder blush with a large makeup brush.*

BRIGHTON *and* VIOLET *come up the back stairway.* VIOLET

carries a tray of enormous corsages. BRIGHTON *is cleaning his jacket with a damp rag)*

BRIGHTON Look, there, I'm stained for the night. I'm just livid. Actually, Ms. Moone, since my Uncle Theodore's death I've tried to assume a refined appearance and a serious manner to show respect for my grandmother's relentless grief. I feel it is my mission in life. I've found that people need a mission. Otherwise there's confusion and if there is one thing we all must avoid, Ms. Moone, that is confusion.

VIOLET There's a whole mess of that going on.

BRIGHTON Yes, indeed, and it's not to be trifled with.

(BLISS *and* FRANCES *come out of the bathroom into the parlor)*

Oh, horrors!

BLISS (*To* FRANCES) Just ignore him.

BRIGHTON I'm stuffing the cleaning bill for this down your throat.

(BRIGHTON *turns away.* BLISS *sees the corsages)*

BLISS Why, look! The corsages have arrived! The bouquets for our breasts.

VIOLET (*To* BLISS) Here's yours right here. It's the biggest one of all. I guess someone must adore you a whole lot.

BLISS Well, yes, I sent it to myself. What I love most about corsages is the fact that they're so very, very beautiful for only one night. How special that makes the one night.

(FRANCES *is excitedly smelling all of the flowers. She picks up* TEDDY's *bouquet, then puts it back)*

VIOLET Here, Frances, this one's for you.

> (FRANCES *takes the corsage with delight, then starts to pin it on* VIOLET)

Oh no, it's not for me.

> (FRANCES *picks up the bouquet and offers it*)

BLISS No, Frances. Violet doesn't get a corsage. She's not going. She's the maid.

> (TEDDY *comes rushing in from the main stairway. She is white with fear and is pulling at her hairpiece*)

TEDDY Oh, Lord—Oh, Lord. No, no. I can't go. I can't go to the fancy ball.

BRIGHTON Teddy, what's wrong? Are you all right?

TEDDY Grandmother says I look just like my daddy. She says I'm his splitting image.

> (*Looking into her veins*)

She says she can see the Parker blood inside me. She can see it!

BLISS Oh, that old bitch is blind as a bat.

TEDDY I think I'd better not go. I think there are rats inside my hairpiece.

BRIGHTON We're in trouble. Big trouble.

TEDDY (*Running on*) Rats! Rats! I knew it all along. I'd better not go.

> (TEDDY *exits into the bathroom and slams the door shut*)

BLISS Darling Teddy, always looking at the world through rose-colored glasses.

> (JEN *bursts into the room. She carries* TEDDY's *cape and evening bag. In the bathroom,* TEDDY *starts pulling apart her hairpiece*)

JEN Where's Teddy. Where'd she go? Bliss?!

(BLISS *indicates the bathroom*)

BLISS Le toilette.

JEN Please, everyone, get yourselves together. We've got to leave here this minute. I mean it, everyone! This minute! Violet, run over to my room and bring me my sable fur, it's lying out on the bed.

(BLISS *and* FRANCES *go up the stairs.* VIOLET *exits to* JEN'S *room.* JEN *goes into the bathroom with* TEDDY. BRIGHTON *exits down the main stairway*)

JEN Teddy, what are you doing?

TEDDY (*Pulling at her hair*) Do you see any rats in here? I thought I saw some rats.

JEN Jesus, child, are you having a breakdown?

TEDDY Am I? I could be. I don't know. I wish Daddy were here. See, otherwise, they'll all look at me and it'll just remind them of how he died and how he can't be here tonight.

JEN Look, Teddy, even if your daddy had survived he wouldn't be here tonight. He would have been convicted of embezzlement and fraud. He'd be stuck in jail for life.

TEDDY Alive though. He'd be alive.

JEN Let it go, Teddy. Please. There's nothing left I can do. Let it go.

TEDDY It just sticks in my mind how Daddy brought me that Peter Rabbit coloring book after my thumb got smashed.

JEN Well, does it also stick in your mind how he smashed your thumb and how he poured scalding chili over my head and what he did to the goldfish?

TEDDY He wasn't a well man. I know that. Oh, Mama, it just won't ever heal up. It's raw scabs over raw scabs and now it's all ripping away.

JEN Teddy, don't do this. Not now.

TEDDY They're all gonna see through me. Inside me.

(HANK *enters the parlor from the main stairway*)

HANK (*Yelling*) Hey, people! Let's get this show on the road! Jen?! Hey, Jen!

JEN (*From bathroom*) Yes, darling! We're coming!

HANK Well, Theadora's being wheeled out to her car right now. She wants Teddy to ride in there with her!

JEN (*Rapidly trying to do something with* TEDDY's *torn-down hair*) We'll be right there!

HANK (*Pouring a drink*) Okay, but you'd better hurry. The roads to hell are paved with the skulls of unpresented debutantes!

TEDDY Why did you have to marry him?

JEN I needed help. We had no money. I couldn't let you take that job in the school cafeteria. You'd never have gotten into a proper sorority.

TEDDY I didn't care. I would have done the work. I would have done anything not to lose you again, or hurt you. Hurt you to help me. Oh, my face. My face.

(TEDDY *pulls away from* JEN, *and rushes to the toilet to vomit.* JEN *wets a towel and goes to wash* TEDDY's *face*)

JEN God, Teddy. How much have you been drinking? Are you going to be all right?

TEDDY Uh-huh. It's just . . . Mama, I'm pregnant.

(J E N *stares at her wide-eyed*)

H A N K (*Looking at his watch*) Hey, as a personal favor to me, could we all head out of here before the goddamned sunrise!?

J E N Whose is it? Is it that boy's from Atlanta? Is it that David Brickman's?

T E D D Y There isn't any David Brickman from Atlanta. I just made him up.

J E N What?

T E D D Y I was gonna be dead by now, it wasn't gonna matter. But now I gotta wait for this thing to be born. Even though I know it's going to be born horrible.

H A N K Let's move out! Roll 'em, roll 'em, roll 'em!

> (J E N *starts singing "We Wish You a Merry Christmas" in a frantic whisper, as she works with* T E D D Y's *hair*)

Hey, everyone! Let's get organized. Roll 'em, people! Roll 'em!

> (B R I G H T O N *enters from the main stairway*)

B R I G H T O N Grandmother's waiting on all of y'all down in her car.

H A N K Relax. Settle down!

B R I G H T O N This is extremely rude.

H A N K Relax. The night is young.

> (H A N K *heads for the bar. He knocks into the silver vase of party favors causing the vase to tumble to the floor. Sparkling colored prizes spill out across the rug.* J E N *stops singing*)

Ah, Hell's fire! All the goddamn party favors. If I'm not the clumsiest man ever put on God's earth.

> (H A N K *kneels down on the floor and starts sweeping the prizes back into the silver vase*)

(BLISS *and* FRANCES *come down the stairs carrying their wraps and evening bags*)

BLISS Oh, look at the treasures! The treasures.

(BLISS *picks up a paper crown covered with glitter that is among the party favors*)

A princess's crown!

(HANK *turns away from them, then turns back towards them wearing a red nose that fell from the silver vase*)

HANK Honk. Honk.

(JEN *and* TEDDY *enter the parlor from the bathroom.* TEDDY *wears her cape and her tiara; her hair is a mess.* FRANCES *picks up a gold fan*)

JEN Oh, no, Hank, those party favors were to be given out after the ball.

HANK No problem. We'll put 'em all back.

JEN We're going, everyone, now!

(*To* HANK)

Oh, Hank, come here.

(*She takes the red nose off of* HANK *and drops it into the silver vase*)

BRIGHTON (*Overlapping, to* TEDDY) Teddy, you and I are riding with Grandmother. We must hurry. They're out there waiting.

BLISS (*Overlapping*) Teddy, dear, what's happened to your hair? You've destroyed your hair.

JEN She's going to fix it in the car.

BRIGHTON (*To* TEDDY, *handing her the debutante bouquet and a corsage*) Teddy, these are for you. You'll have to pin them on in the car.

(*To everyone*)

Hurry up! Hurry up! Everyone's waiting.

HANK (*Overlapping, to* BLISS *and* FRANCES. *They both keep their party favors*)

My, what a lucky man I am tonight, escorting all these beautiful dolls to the Hattiesburg Debutante Ball.

> (BRIGHTON, TEDDY, HANK, BLISS *and* FRANCES *all exit out the hall door as* JEN *talks rapidly to* VIOLET *while pinning on her corsage*)

JEN (*Overlapping*) We'll be returning about two a.m. so be sure the canapes are prepared and the bar is set up. You can heat up the hot hors d'oeuvres after we've arrived.

VIOLET All right.

> (*Helping* JEN *into her fur coat*)

My, this is a fine silky fur.

JEN Don't worry, Violet, when you're my age, you'll have a fur that's just as fine and just as silky and you will have earned every goddamned hair on it. Just like I have. 'Bye-bye now.

VIOLET 'Bye.

> (JEN *exits out the hall door*)

> (*Blackout*)

Act II

SCENE ONE

*Finger sandwiches, various canapes and exotic cheeses have been
put out on silver platters.*

*TEDDY appears walking barefoot along the balcony railing,
swinging her cape. Her dress is torn and dirty. She no longer
wears the hairpiece.*

TEDDY Clang! Clang! Clang! I'm not a bell. Not a bell! No bell.

(*TEDDY jumps off the balcony railing and comes into the room.
She is crazed with jubilation.*)

Look, one cheese knife.

(*Her eye catches the cheese knife. She picks it up and starts slash-
ing at her face.*)

Okay. Fine. Face. The face. Face. Whole face.

(*VIOLET enters from the back stairs with a tray. She slings the
tray aside and knocks the knife out of TEDDY's hand*)

VIOLET What you wanna do? Look here, there's blood.

TEDDY (*With a fierce crazed triumph*) Violet, I'm no belle. Mama,
she wanted me to go to that ball and be a belle. But me, I'm no belle.

VIOLET (*Handing TEDDY a napkin*) There now. Hold that to the
cut.

TEDDY Awhile ago, see, I was staying by myself at an old hotel up in Oxford, Mississippi. After supper one night I got on the elevator to ride up to my room. And just as the doors were about to close, a man stepped inside to ride up with me. I glanced over and saw his left arm was cut off right above the elbow. He wore a short-sleeved shirt and you could see the scarred nub. Then I caught sight of his face where the whole side of it was just . . . missing. I felt sick and sticky, and wanted to get off the ride. My legs buckled out from under me; he reached his good arm out to help me up. But I said to him, "You get away from me, you ugly man." Then the elevator stopped. The doors opened. But he didn't move. He just stayed hovering over in a corner with this weepy cry coming from inside his throat.

VIOLET Uh-huh. Well, I'm sure it wasn't the first time people turned scared on him and caused his feelings to be injured. I reckon he'd better get used to it.

TEDDY Violet, do you remember that baby I spoke to you about?

VIOLET Yeah.

TEDDY It's his baby.

VIOLET The bad-looking one on the elevator?

TEDDY Uh huh. I kinda just did it to be polite. I was at a point, you see, where I couldn't take on any more, ah, bad feelings, guilt. Just no more.

     (TEDDY *offers a cigarette from a Band-Aid box*)

Wanna smoke?

VIOLET No thanks.

     (TEDDY *sniffs*)

TEDDY After we did it he said to me, "Mm-mm good." Can you believe it? "Mm-mm good."

VIOLET Kinda like you was M&M's or somptin'.

TEDDY Yeah. I still smell him on my skin sometimes.

(*She sniffs*)

God. I gotta stop that.

VIOLET What?

TEDDY Sniffing. I sniff when I'm afraid.

VIOLET What are you afraid of?

TEDDY (*A chill runs through her*) Hidden things.

(*She sniffs*)

Did you ever have hidden things?

VIOLET I used to write secrets in jars and bury the jars outside in the dirt.

TEDDY What kinda secrets did you bury?

VIOLET Different things I had to get off'a my chest.

TEDDY I know how that feels. On your chest. I've got things on my chest.

VIOLET What things?

TEDDY Certain acts. Irredeemable acts.

(*Honking horns and screeching cars are heard*)

Wait! Wait! Oh, it's them. Look, there they are. Brighton's jumping out of the limousine heading for the front door swinging his cane.

VIOLET Oh, yeah. And there's the rest of 'em pulling up behind. Why, who's that leaning outta the window? Looks like they's getting sick to their stomach.

TEDDY That's Frances. I recognize the cape. Oh, there's Mama. Look at her shaking her fists up at the sky.

BRIGHTON'S VOICE (*Offstage*) Teddy! Teddy, are you here?

TEDDY She's not gonna want me now. She's through with me. Finished.

(BRIGHTON *comes into the room from the main stairway*)

BRIGHTON There you are! Thank God I found you before your mother caught up with you.

TEDDY I bet she wants me dead.

BRIGHTON What happened to your face?

TEDDY There was a dreadful accident.

BRIGHTON Christ. Listen to me, Teddy, I spoke to Grandmother Theadora tonight. She's aware of the damage Aunt Jen inflicted on you by forcing you to lie for her at the trial; saying she acted in self defense. Everyone saw there wasn't a mark on her.

JEN'S VOICE (*Offstage*) Teddy! Teddy! Theadora Jenniquade!

(VIOLET *exits down the back stairway*)

BRIGHTON Grandmother wants you to come live with her. She wants to give you a chance to get away from your mother and regain your, well, your sanity.

JEN'S VOICE (*Offstage*) Teddy! Are you here in this house? Are you here?

BRIGHTON In my opinion it's your only hope.

JEN'S VOICE (*Offstage*) Teddy!

TEDDY Yes, I'll go. You tell her though. You break the news.

(TEDDY *disappears out onto the balcony.*

JEN *and* BLISS *burst into the room from the main stairway.*

JEN *searches through the second floor calling for* TEDDY.

BLISS *helps half-heartedly*)

JEN Teddy! Teddy!

BLISS Teddy! Teddy Bear.

JEN Teddy! Teddy! She's not here. God, to think I've always feared an early death. Christ, if only I'd had one!

BLISS You can't make silk purses out of sow's ears.

JEN (*Lighting up a cigarette from a package she keeps stuck under her garter*) But why act like a banshee? Why destroy all I've done for her?

BRIGHTON Perhaps, if you hadn't brought along that professional boor you call a husband, we could have managed to escape with some small semblance of dignity.

BLISS Not after Teddy made her first bow with her gown pulled up over her head and two feet of toilet paper stuck to her slipper.

JEN Oh, and then later I found her crawling under the banquet table smearing cream cheese onto people's shoes.

BRIGHTON Was that before or after Hank broke Mrs. Carver's toe when he waltzed?

JEN After. It was right before he instigated that horrific brawl. I started searching all over for Teddy as soon as I discovered her hairpiece floating in the punch bowl.

BLISS Disgusting.

BRIGHTON Yes, but the most pathetic display was how Mrs. Rover kept pumping that idiot *Frances* for information about the reconciliation of our families.

BLISS Poor Frances. Everyone knew she'd fallen right off the turnip truck. No one even asked her to dance.

JEN When I find that girl I'm going to shake her till her teeth fall out of her face. How could she do this to me?! It's inexcusable! Everything was rehearsed!

(HANK *and* VIOLET *burst in from the main stairway.* HANK's *shirt is torn, his face is bruised. He no longer wears his bow tie or jacket. They are lugging in* FRANCES *who is sprawled all over the place. She drags* TEDDY's *white stole along after her. It is covered with champagne, dirt and vomit*)

HANK That's right, get her in here. Watch out for her head.

JEN Oh, God.　　　　　　　　BRIGHTON Oh, my.

(JEN *runs to the bathroom to get a towel.* BRIGHTON *grabs a wastepaper can*)

HANK Lay her over here. Sit her up. She might choke herself like that.

VIOLET Gee, she looks bad.

HANK Frances, Baby? It's your Uncle Hank, here. Hey, are you gonna be okay?

(JEN *enters from the bathroom*)

FRANCES ''YES, I—I—. WHAT WILL MAMA SAY?''

HANK Huh?

FRANCES ''NO ONE MARRIED ME! NO ONE ASKED ME TO DANCE.''

HANK I'm sorry, I don't understand what you're saying.

FRANCES ''WHEN MAMA—WHEN SHE DIES, SHE'LL KNOW I'M AN OLD MAID. NO ONE ASKED ME TO DANCE!''

HANK Please, Baby.

FRANCES ''OH, LOOK! I RUINED TEDDY'S CAPE! LOOK! MAYBE I CAN WASH OUT. YES. LET IT WASH OUT.''

(FRANCES *runs into the bathroom and starts trying to clean* TEDDY'S *soiled cape.* VIOLET *follows after her*)

HANK God, I hate it when I can't understand what she's trying to say. I just hate it.

BLISS She was saying no one asked her to dance and she ruined Teddy's cape.

HANK Oh, yeah, well, I got that part t'do with Teddy's cape. So, ah, how about Teddy? Has anyone heard from her?

BLISS No, she just ran off into the night. She does that very well, running off into the night.

JEN It's a family trait.

HANK Hmm. So, some party, eh? But look, folks, if we were always gonna do everything perfect, why bother being born, right?

(BLISS *and* BRIGHTON *voice general groans of despair*)

JEN Yeah, right.

HANK Hey, do I detect a pall of doom?

(*To* JEN)

Please, what can I do to make you happy? Hey now! Could I do a jig?!

(HANK *does a silly jig.*

HANK *flips the top of his toupee up and down several times.*

JEN *screams in disgust and rises to her feet*)

Please, Jen, any fall from your grace is unbearable to me. Look, I'm sorry about that scuffle.

JEN Scuffle?! You broke a man's nose, tore up half the ballroom and destroyed a whole event!

HANK I didn't like how some of those people were treating us.

JEN Do you think I did? Christ, I picked up a butter knife at the buffet table and everyone fled in horror. God knows it wasn't easy being the only murderess at the ball. But I stood there and stood it and smiled. I did it for Teddy. God, how could she betray me like that?

BRIGHTON Listen, Aunt Jen, about Teddy, well, Grandmother Theadora was very upset about how things went tonight.

(VIOLET *and* FRANCES *enter the main room from the bathroom*)

JEN Oh, really, Brighton. How surprising. Violet, please pass around the hors d'oeuvres.

BRIGHTON She, well, Grandmother, honestly feels Teddy's future is in grave jeopardy if she stays, well, with you. I, ah, spoke to Teddy and she agreed to go live with Grandmother for a time.

JEN Brighton, why are you telling me such useless lies? Don't you think I know my own daughter?

BRIGHTON No, not particularly.

(*He calls out the balcony door*)

Teddy! Teddy, will you come in here, please! I need your corroboration.

JEN Is she out there? Is she here?

(BRIGHTON *enters with* TEDDY. TEDDY *keeps her head down*)

JEN Teddy, Teddy, look at me. Look at me. What happened to your face?

TEDDY It broke out. I ate a lot of chocolate and it's all broken out.

BRIGHTON Just look at her, Aunt Jen. You've done this to her. You've made her crazy. Go on, tell her, Teddy. Tell your mother you're going to stay with Grandmother from now on.

JEN Yes, tell me, Teddy. Tell me that.

TEDDY I thought it might be an idea.

JEN I see.

> (JEN *goes out onto the balcony. There is a long moment of* *silence.* BLISS *moves up to* TEDDY)

BLISS (*To* TEDDY) She's mad at you. You're nothing but a disappointment. She hates the sight of you.

> (BLISS *moves away from* TEDDY. *After a moment* JEN *enters from the balcony*)

JEN Teddy, will you just tell me one thing? Where has my enchanted child gone?

TEDDY I don't know, Mama.

JEN Why do you want to leave me? Haven't we always been closest of friends?

TEDDY I thought you'd want me gone.

JEN No. Oh, no. You're all I've got that's good. If I lose you, I have nothing. You're all the hope I have left.

BLISS What about me, Mama? Don't you care anything for me? For moi? I'm not just some sack of garbage. I'm your oldest child. I inherited your elegance. I resemble you in every way. She—She looks like some drowned rat.

JEN Bliss, don't start in on this. Not tonight.

BLISS You're obviously jealous of my angelic beauty. That's why you shun and neglect me.

JEN Neglect you? I neglect you? Well, please, let us not forget about little Butterball when we speak of neglected children. When was the last time you saw your child? What did you send her for her birthday? I never once have forgotten *your* birthday. Although I wish to God I could!

BLISS Christ, why didn't they keep you in jail? I wish they'd stuck you in a hole forever! I hate you!

JEN You! You think I could be jealous of you! You dream you're some beautiful lady, but you're nothing but a Southern strumpet whore!

BLISS Oh really, Mama, well, fuck you!

JEN You! You bring all your filthy baggage in here to intrude on my life, but I'm throwing you out! Out! Do you hear me! Out! Out! Out!

BLISS (*Overlapping*) Fuck you, Mother. Just fuck you! Fuck you! Fuck you dead!

JEN You're an unproductive being! A worthless mis-creation! You're cheap! Cheap! Cheap!

(BLISS *can no longer endure the abuse. She flees up the stairs*)

BLISS *Aahh! Aahh!* No more!

(BLISS *trips on the stairs and falls.* FRANCES *rushes up to her*)

FRANCES ''OH BLISS! DEAR BLISS!''

BLISS *Ugh!* Look at you! There's green food between your teeth! You ugly, ugly thing! Get away from me! Keep away!

(FRANCES *flees into the bathroom to brush her teeth.* BLISS *exits up the stairway*)

JEN Maybe I'm not a very good mother. Maybe I never should have had any children after all.

BRIGHTON Your wife's insane.

HANK I know. I'm aware of it all.

JEN Teddy, go put on some shoes. Pack some things. We're leaving here tonight.

TEDDY Leaving tonight?

JEN I'm getting you out of this town for good. I don't like these people influencing you. Move! Do you hear me?! Move! Move!

BRIGHTON (*Overlapping*) What are you so afraid of, Aunt Jen? Christ, no one's trying to get Teddy to reverse her testimony. Besides, they can't try you twice for the same murder.

JEN (*To* TEDDY; *running on*) And put on some makeup. Your face is a mess. Fix it right!

(TEDDY *exits to her bedroom*)

BRIGHTON (*Overlapping*) Teddy! Teddy! Aunt Jen, you can't do this. I'm calling Grandmother.

JEN Not from my house. Get out of my house. I'll rip you to shreds. I know how it's done.

BRIGHTON You can be sure there are measures we can take.

JEN Violet, show my nephew to the door. Don't let him lose his way.

BRIGHTON I'll be back. I'll be back tonight.

(VIOLET *and* BRIGHTON *exit down the main stairway*)

JEN Hank. Oh, Hank, we've got to leave here right away. I hate this town! I hate these people! I'd like to chop up every dreadful one of them and burn them all to ash ruins!

HANK Sure, I understand. Things didn't go—the way you'd hoped. Look, I'll make us a reservation at the Hotel Royal. We can stay there a week. Let things settle down.

JEN You don't understand. I don't want to go to New Orleans for a week's vacation. I want to move away from here for good. God, I just wish I knew—I just wish I knew where we'd—fit in. Let's see. Have you ever been to Pennsylvania? How about Delaware? Or, or Maine? Yes, Maine's way, way up there, isn't it? We could do well in Maine.

HANK Jen, we can't just pick up and move lock, stock and barrel. All my work's here. And this house. Christ, I just spent three fortunes building you this huge, enormous house. You said you loved this house.

JEN I don't love it. I don't. I want to go away. We'll never be able to live in this town. It was foolish to try. I'll go get my jewels. We'll hire movers to handle the rest.

(JEN *starts up the stairs to get her jewels*)

HANK Jen, please. You're overwrought. Your rational mind has gone askew.

JEN You don't understand. Teddy's in trouble. She's pregnant.

HANK Ah, Lord.

JEN We'll have to get rid of it. I won't let her life be ruined like mine was, but we can't do it here. We'll take care of all that up in Maine.

HANK Have you talked to Teddy about this? What does she want to do?

JEN She wants what I want.

HANK Have you asked her?

JEN Look, Teddy's surrounded by people that are breaking her down, turning her against me. I've got to get her safe. And if you won't help me, I'll go without you.

HANK Look, we're married. We stay together. You can't go without me.

JEN Yes, I can. Don't think you can hold me here. I own all of the jewelry upstairs in that safe. It's registered in my name. I saw to it this time that I wouldn't be left holding nothing.

HANK Is that what you think? That I'd leave you holding nothing?

When have I ever been cheap with you? Why, I've given you everything your blood-cold bitch heart's desired. You've used me up real good.

JEN I never asked you for all of your help and salvation. I didn't want to end up owing you a whole lot of blood I could never pay back.

HANK Don't worry, Jen, you don't owe me a goddamn thing. Not blood or nothing. You're free and clear. Go on. Go! Oh, wait. All the jewelry's yours, right? Well, here's my watch. Take it.

> (*He slings it at her*)

And my ring. And these; they're all yours.

> (*He slings his cuff links at her*)

Live it up! Here, take some silver with you! It's a bonus prize!

> (**HANK** *slings a sliver tray and goblets across the room*)

JEN Look at you! Just look! You're nothing but a redneck bull. God, am I sick of trying to keep you penned in.

HANK Nothing worked, did it? The new clothes, the toupee, the fancy manicure. Christ, you even changed my toothpaste brand and deodorant bar. Tell me, wasn't there anything about me you could stand besides my money?

JEN No, there was nothing. Nothing at all.

HANK Which car do you want to take with you?

JEN We'll take the Lincoln.

HANK Alright. I'll go get it out of the garage and pull it around front for you.

> (**HANK** *exits down the main stairway.* **JEN** *goes into the bathroom where* **FRANCES** *is sitting at the dressing table scrubbing her teeth with a wash rag*)

JEN You! This is my bathroom. Get out! I've got to pack. I'm through with all of you. Leave me alone.

(FRANCES *flees into the main room.* JEN *slings various random toilet articles into a quilted bag, then exits into her bedroom.* VIOLET *comes up the back stairway with a large tray.* FRANCES *sees her and starts to head up the stairs.*

VIOLET *begins picking up various hors d'oeuvre plates.*

FRANCES *haughtily motions to* VIOLET *to pour her a glass of champagne.* VIOLET *pours the wine.* FRANCES *demands her to fill the glass.* VIOLET *fills the glass.*

FRANCES *slings the wine into* VIOLET's *face.* VIOLET *exits down the back stairway.* FRANCES *walks around the room with a sense of gloating victory. After a few moments her sense of triumph turns to regretful despair. She sinks to the floor in anguish.* BLISS *comes down the stairway. She is taking a pill and humming a sad French song. Without noticing* FRANCES, *she goes to the phone and dials*)

BLISS (*Into phone*) Yes, hello? Is this Tommy? . . . Well, hi, this is Blissy. I'm, oh, just visiting here in town for a while . . . Yes, right, for Teddy's Debutante Ball. How's my little girl? How's Butterball—did she know I was going to the ball? . . . Oh, well, anyway tell her I'm going to give her the jeweled princess's crown I received as a party favor. I want her to have it . . . Listen, Tommy, could I, ah, could I come see you sometime? . . . Well, it's just, I—I miss you and Butterball an awful lot, and I'd really like to maybe—try and come back home . . . Right. Well, of course, I know it's very difficult to live with me day in

and day out . . . It's just I can't seem to make it on my own. My last employer accused me of lying about graduating from high school. He said I couldn't make change properly. I've got to tell you, I just don't know what's going to become of me . . . Yes. Certainly, I understand how you feel . . . Uh-huh. I see . . . No, really it was just a—fleeting fancy I had. You see, it occurred to me that I'd be able to teach Butterball how to tell time and tie her shoe. I didn't learn how to do those two things until very late and I remember feeling so badly about it . . . You will? Well, good then. That's very good. So, Tommy, goodbye.

> (BLISS *puts the phone down.*
>
> *With a laugh*)

Oh, well, maybe it was a mistake sleeping with every one of his friends before leaving the state.

> (BLISS *goes to the tape player and punches a button. A Chopin*
> *waltz plays.* BLISS *turns off the light, dances alone then spots*
> FRANCES *who is sitting on the floor staring at her*)

Look, I'm sorry I said that about the green in your teeth.

FRANCES "LOOK HERE. IT'S GONE."

BLISS Yes. I'm sorry. I don't mean to be cruel. I just have this sort of hole inside me. This desperate longing to love and be loved. Somehow it cripples me. It makes me be cruel.

FRANCES "YES. LOVE. HOLE."

BLISS Yes. You understand me. I can talk to you.

> (BLISS *touches* FRANCES *softly. The moment is very potent.*
>
> BLISS *gets up and runs to the balcony.* FRANCES *follows her*)

Oh, smell that night grass. I love t'smell nice things.

(*They smell the grass. Then gently, slowly, they begin dancing together.*

BLISS; *still dancing*)

Look at the moon. A rose pink moon.

FRANCES (*Touching* BLISS' *lips*) "IT'S RED . . . IT'S RED JUST LIKE YOUR LIPS."

(BLISS *reaches for* FRANCES' *hand. She kisses the palm of it softly. Then she holds* FRANCES' *hand in hers as she kisses* FRANCES *full on the lips.* BLISS *continues kissing* FRANCES *passionately on the neck and shoulders, as she feels the fullness of her breasts*)

BLISS Yes, just two lost souls dancing on the rooftop together.

(BLISS *pulls* FRANCES *to the floor as she unzips her dress.* JEN *enters the parlor from her room. She has changed out of her gown into traveling clothes. She wears her mink coat and carries a suitcase. She turns on the light and sees* BLISS *and* FRANCES)

JEN Oh, and I thought they considered that something of a taboo down in this part of the state.

(FRANCES *leaps up and rushes off down the back stairway.* BLISS *gets up and looks after* FRANCES. JEN *starts up the stairs*)

Cheap. You're cheap, cheap, cheap.

BLISS That's not true. I don't believe you anymore. It's not true.

(JEN *exits up the stairs.* BLISS *exits out onto the balcony.*

TEDDY *enters from the hallway. She wears her debutante gown with black loafers and carries a round makeup bag*

VIOLET *enters from the back stairway. She has changed into a worn-out fraternity T-shirt, polyester pants and a worn-down pair of shoes.)*

VIOLET   I'm ready to go home.

TEDDY   Alright. We'll take you. We're going, too.

(TEDDY *gets a cheese knife, pulls up her skirt and cuts her leg)*

VIOLET   I can't get involved with you people no more.

TEDDY   I'm just slicing away at it. That's all I can do for now. After I have the child of the elevator man, then I can stop it for good. Violet, have you ever wanted to stop it for good?

VIOLET   I did one time. It was after my mama died eating them left-over lunch meat sandwiches this white lady'd given over to her. I felt such hatred inside my heart I went out wild on the streets and stole whatever I wanted and didn't have. They caught me and I paid my time. Now I'm starting new.

TEDDY   Me; I can't start new. No way. I got too many things on my chest. I keep trying to push them down, but they keep gripping back up at me.

VIOLET   Just like an old snapping turtle.

TEDDY   Huh?

VIOLET   A snapping turtle. They don't never let loose till it thunders.

TEDDY   But it never does thunder. I got all this lightning inside me. But it won't ever thunder.

VIOLET   Then you make it thunder. You make it. Ya don't wanna end up like my brother. He just laid himself down on a railroad track and died.

TEDDY   Why'd he do that?

VIOLET I guess he just couldn't see no other way.

(*After a moment* JEN *comes hurrying down the staircase with her jewels*)

JEN Teddy, are you packed? Teddy?

TEDDY (*Turning to her*) Mama—

JEN What?

TEDDY I can't go.

JEN Why not?

TEDDY I'm afraid.

JEN What do you mean? Afraid of what?

TEDDY Afraid of you.

JEN Christ. Jesus Christ. How can that be? I've given up everything for you. Everything.

TEDDY Don't give up any more. I don't want it.

JEN Yes you do. You're in trouble. You need help. I'll get you a doctor. We'll fix it. It won't be a problem.

TEDDY But it is a problem. It is.

BRIGHTON (*Offstage*) Teddy! Teddy!

HANK (*Offstage*) Get out! I'll tear your head off!

BRIGHTON (*Offstage*) Stay away from me! Get away! Teddy!

(HANK *and* BRIGHTON *come racing up the front stairway*)

JEN (*Overlapping*) Don't let him in here! Keep him out!

BRIGHTON Take your hands off—

HANK I'm sick of dealing with you people.

(HANK *slings* BRIGHTON *across the room*)

HANK All of you. I mean all of you.

BRIGHTON Teddy, Grandmother's outside in her car.

JEN Hank. Get him out. Hank—

(HANK *starts up the stairs*)

BRIGHTON She wants to talk to you.

JEN She's not talking to anyone.

TEDDY Yes I am. There's something I have to say.

JEN You are not saying anything. You're coming with me.

TEDDY No way, no way. I'm having this baby. I'm not gonna kill it too. I'm not killing anybody anymore.

BRIGHTON Teddy, what do you mean?

JEN Don't listen to her. She's utterly deluded. She's having a breakdown. Leave her alone.

TEDDY (*Overlapping*) I'm not afraid of telling anymore. I'm sorry, Mama. I'm past afraid.

JEN Shut up! You'll ruin all I've done for you. You'll destroy your whole life! Don't do this to me!

TEDDY (*Overlapping*) Give up, Mama. You can't stop me. You never could.

BRIGHTON (*Overlapping*) Teddy, what is it? What are you saying?

TEDDY I'm saying how I did it. I smashed Daddy with that black pan and he fell over into his turnip greens cold dead. It was me that killed him. It was me that smashed him dead!

BRIGHTON (*Overlapping*) Christ. Oh Christ.

JEN (*Overlapping as she violently shakes* TEDDY)
She's a liar! She's smoking again too! She says she doesn't smoke but she does! I know it! I've smelt it on her.

(*She begins slapping* TEDDY *repeatedly. She slings her across a chaise lounge*)

You liar! Traitor! Shut up! Shut up your mouth! I'll knock it off! I'll shut it up for good!

(HANK *pulls* JEN *away*)

HANK God, stop, Jen. Christ, stop!

(TEDDY *groans in agony as blood falls into the lap of her white gown*)

TEDDY Oh no! Oh no! I knew it would be born horrible!

JEN (*Overlapping*) My God. My God.

BRIGHTON Holy God. Please, please.

(HANK *rushes to* TEDDY *and holds her in his arms*)

HANK It's all right, Teddy. Call the hospital. It'll be all right.

(BRIGHTON *goes to the phone*)

TEDDY (*Reaching her arms out to* JEN) Mama!! I want my Mama! Please, Mama!

JEN (*Overlapping*) Yes. Alright. Okay.

(JEN *goes to the floor and takes* TEDDY *in her arms.* HANK *moves away from them*)

I'm here, baby. I'm right here.

(*Blackout*)

SCENE TWO

It is early the following morning. FRANCES *is sitting on the sofa in her dusty traveling clothes staring out into space. Her suitcase sits by the stairway.* VIOLET *enters from the back stairway with a breakfast tray. She looks exhausted. She sets the tray down on the coffee table.*

FRANCES *looks up at* VIOLET *and then hides her face.* VIOLET *looks at her and turns away.* HANK *enters from* JEN'S *bedroom carrying a large suitcase.*

HANK Violet, hello. Thanks for getting the breakfast. Listen, soon as Teddy comes back from the hospital we'll be heading up to Pontotoc. My sister Sue's taken a turn for the worse. I'll drop you home on the way.

VIOLET Good.

HANK (*Handing her an enormous wad of money*) Look, ah, here's your money. I'm adding in a little extra for all the inconveniences we've caused you. I apologize for everything. I'm deeply embarrassed 'bout all those events happening. But people in this world'll love each other and hate each other—you never know which; there's a wonderment to it all.

VIOLET Yeah, well, I'll go down and get my things so I can go home.

HANK Okay.

(VIOLET *exits down the back stairway.* HANK *sits down with* FRANCES)

Hey, how ya doing?

(*He takes the silver cover off of the breakfast plate*)

Mmm. Look here what we've got for breakfast this morning. Lotsa good fresh eggs and sausage. Here, try some.

(FRANCES *shakes her head*)

Well, how 'bout some hot grits? I know you like your grits. Here, we'll fix it up for you with a load of butter; and then give it some good ole salt and pepper. Yeah. Now stir it all around. There you go.

(HANK *offers her the bowl of grits.* FRANCES *shakes her head*)

FRANCES "YOU'RE VERY NICE, UNCLE HANK, BUT I JUST DO NOT FEEL HUNGRY."

HANK What? Not enough butter? Here, we'll add more butter. I like mine buttery too. Now, come on now. Ya gotta eat something. It's a long drive home. A really long drive all the way t' Pontotoc.

FRANCES "PLEASE, I DON'T WANT IT. PLEASE!"

HANK Well, look, then you don't have to eat it. Here, I can go on and eat it myself. Hell, it's fixed just like I like it.

(HANK *takes a big bite of grits.* BLISS *enters the parlor from the main stairway. She still wears her evening gown*)

BLISS Hi, we're back.

HANK Bliss, hi. Where's Teddy?

BLISS She's downstairs. I think she feels a little weak. Maybe you should help carry her up to her room.

HANK Alright. Good. Be glad to.

(HANK *exits down the main stairway*)

BLISS Hi.

FRANCES ''HI.''

BLISS I heard they called about your mother.

FRANCES ''YES.''

BLISS She's . . . doing poorly.

FRANCES ''YES. VERY.''

BLISS I'm so sorry.

  (*A beat*)

Frances.

FRANCES ''HUH?''

BLISS I hope I didn't—I mean last night—I guess, I just . . . like you very much.

FRANCES ''YOU DO?''

BLISS Uh huh. I do. Yes.

FRANCES ''OH.''

BLISS Yes.

FRANCES ''BLISS?''

BLISS Yes?

FRANCES ''WHEN I GO HOME—''

BLISS Home.

FRANCES ''YES, I'D LIKE—I MEAN IF YOU—IT'S JUST—''

BLISS What? What?

FRANCES ''BLISS, WOULD YOU WANT TO GO HOME WITH ME?''

BLISS Enchante. Delightful. Yes.

FRANCES ''GOOD.''

BLISS Good. Yes. Well, then I've got to run and go change. And pack. I'll—just be a minute.

FRANCES ''I'LL HELP YOU.''

BLISS Help, yes, alright. Thank you. Alright.

>   (BLISS *and* FRANCES *exit up the stairs.* HANK *carries*
>   TEDDY *into the parlor from the main stairway.* TEDDY *wears*
>   *a brand-new quilted robe*)

TEDDY But you really don't need to carry me. I can walk fine. You could pull out your back.

HANK You're light as a feather.

TEDDY (*Seeing breakfast tray*) Oh, look, is that food? I'm starving.

HANK (*Putting her down*) Sure. Here, sit down and eat then. There's a whole plate that's wasting.

>   (*Handing her a plate*)

There you go.

TEDDY Great.

HANK Here, you want some butter on your grits? It's a lot better with butter.

TEDDY Oh, yes. I love butter. And salt and pepper too.

HANK (*Stirring*) Okay. There you go.

>   (*Watching her take a bite*)

Good?

TEDDY Yeah. That's good.

HANK Well . . . good.

TEDDY (*As she eats*) Hank.

HANK Yeah?

TEDDY Did you always know I was guilty of Daddy dying?

HANK Well, now, guilt can only be determined by a jury of your peers in a court of law. But ask me if I knew you did it. Yeah, I knew.

TEDDY Did she tell you?

HANK Lord, no. God, Jen lied every which way. It's just I had my suppositions. Yeah. Though 'course I never knew about the exact circumstances surrounding the deal. I just figured you didn't intend to actually, ah . . .

TEDDY Kill him.

HANK Yeah.

TEDDY (*Putting jam on her toast*) I don't think I did. Maybe. He broke into the house really crazy that evening. He kept yelling about how he was gonna break Mama all up; cut her to stringy pieces. Seems he'd just found out about her filing for divorce. I served him some coffee and turnip greens, trying t' calm him down. But then he slings the sugar bowl at my chest and starts screaming about how there's not enough sugar, it's not full enough and he's sick of scraping the bottom of the bowl—and he's gonna scrape the bottom of her bowl with this switchblade knife he pulls out. Well, I go to get a broom t' clean up the sugar, but then I hear Mama's car. He hears it too and stops yelling and just sits silently eating turnip greens off the blade of his knife. The car door slams and I hear Mama coming up the walk, that's when I just grab the black skillet and walk back over and smash his skull. To stop him. Just t' stop him till she can run away. That's all I wanted—to let her run away.

HANK Sure. That's all you wanted.

TEDDY I cry sometimes thinking how little I miss him.

HANK Hell, there's no way to blame you for doing what you did.

(TEDDY *looks at him, then looks away*)

Nah. I'm just curious about why you went on and hit him the seven more times.

TEDDY I didn't. She did.

HANK What?

TEDDY Yeah. Mama came in and saw what I'd done, but she told me Daddy wasn't really dead. Then she took the pan and kept on hitting him, telling me she was the one that was doing it, that I never did!

HANK (*Wryly amazed*) Jesus, Jen.

TEDDY But we both knew the truth. It was a bad lie to keep between us.

(BLISS *and* FRANCES *come down the stairway. They are carrying* BLISS' *luggage.* BLISS *is dressed for traveling*)

BLISS (*To* FRANCES) No, really, I think I'd be quite marvelous at hoeing the corn and skinning potatoes.

HANK Oh, good, Frances.

BLISS (*Running on*) Why, people in our family are known for their muscular shoulder blades.

HANK (*To* FRANCES) We need t'head out right away.

BLISS (*To* HANK) I'm going too. Frances asked me to come.

HANK Well fine.

(HANK *exits down the main stairway carrying a load of luggage*)

FRANCES "'BYE, TEDDY. I HAD A LOVELY TIME."

TEDDY (*To* FRANCES) Oh, well, thank you for coming.

BLISS (*To* TEDDY, *as she hands her the princess's crown*)

See that Butterball gets this princess's crown. Tell her it's from her mama. Take care, Teddy Bear.

> (BRIGHTON *enters from the main stairway. He wears a suit, but is quite disheveled. He no longer carries the cane*)

BRIGHTON Teddy! Teddy!

TEDDY Goodbye, Bliss.

BLISS Farewell, farewell.

> (BLISS *and* FRANCES *exit down the main stairs*)

BRIGHTON Goodbye. Goodbye.

> (BRIGHTON *turns to* TEDDY)

Teddy, why did you tell Grandmother? Why did you tell her about what you did? Why in the world?

TEDDY I got tired.

BRIGHTON Tired? You got tired? Fine. Well, it was a dreadful mistake. I don't know what she's going to do. She's certainly not going to take you in.

TEDDY Yes, I know, she told me.

BRIGHTON Well, what are you going to do? You can't stay here, with all these—these unhealthy dynamics.

TEDDY Yes. I'd like some time to get on my feet. Could I stay out at your lake cottage till I do that?

BRIGHTON My cottage? Stay out at my cottage?

TEDDY You're not using it, are you?

BRIGHTON No. Oh no. But Grandmother would never approve. She'd consider me a traitor. Good Lord. Good heavens! I don't understand anything. Life! It's a horrible, hopeless mystery chock full of confusion. Oh, well, go pack your things. I'll drive you out to the lake. Let me pull the car around. Confusion. What can you do about it? There it is.

(BRIGHTON *exits down the main stairway and* TEDDY *exits to her bedroom.* JEN *enters up the back stairway. She wears the fur coat.* JEN *looks around the room and shivers.*

HANK *enters from the main stairway)*

HANK Hello, I—

JEN Hank—

HANK I have to get these bags. We're on our way to Pontotoc.

JEN Yes—well—so . . .

HANK So . . .

JEN . . . Do you want me to be gone when you get back?

HANK Whatever.

JEN Well, anyway, my lost angel, you're better off without me.

HANK Yeah, 'cause it's been a constant struggle to prove my worth to you.

JEN I guess there's just some blackness buried so deep inside my chest you never could have pulled it out with a pair of pliers.

HANK God. Then there's only one problem.

JEN What's that?

HANK I won't be able t'see your face sparkle no more.

JEN Oh please . . . Butter me up. Butter me up some more.

(HANK *picks up the bags and exits down the main stairway.* JEN *turns and goes into her bathroom. She is devastated. She turns on the bath water.)*

Oh God. Oh God.

(JEN *throws blue bath crystals into the tub. She stirs the water with her trembling hand and chants.*)

Please, please, please. Stop please, please.

(JEN *leaves the bathroom and goes into her bedroom.*

TEDDY *enters the parlor from her room, dressed in jeans and a shirt, carrying a suitcase. She hears the water running in* JEN'S *bathroom.* TEDDY *sets down her suitcase. She goes out onto the balcony.*

VIOLET *enters up the back stairway. She carries a large tote bag that has "Le Bag" written on it*)

TEDDY Hi.

VIOLET Hi. Ah, is Mr. Turner ready to leave?

JEN Yes. He went downstairs.

VIOLET Alright.

TEDDY (*Glancing out on the balcony*) Oh, look! Look out there!

VIOLET What?

TEDDY A bird.

VIOLET Where?

TEDDY There! Right there, Violet. By the white branch!

VIOLET Oh yeah. Yeah! I see. There it goes! It was green.

TEDDY Uh-huh, green.

(TEDDY *and* VIOLET *look at each other.* VIOLET *turns and exits down the main stairway.*

JEN *enters the bathroom nude with a large towel wrapped around her shoulders. She is trembling like a new born bird. She walks over to the tub and puts her hand in the water to feel the temperature. She turns off the running water, drops the towel and gets into the tub.*

TEDDY, who hears the water stop, walks over to the door and goes inside the room)

TEDDY Hello.

JEN Teddy.

TEDDY Your psoriasis has broken out again.

JEN I know. It's spreading.

(*Looking at her skin*)

God, look how the ravages of time have conquered me. All these cracks and sores and ugliness. I hate it so much. Being trapped inside this—body.

TEDDY You need to visit that doctor up in Memphis again. Where's your tube of medicine?

JEN On the counter.

(*TEDDY gets the tube and JEN's compact case that holds the cigarettes*)

TEDDY You wanna smoke?

JEN Sure. Let's have a smoke.

(*TEDDY lights a cigarette and hands it to JEN. She lights another one for herself. Then she gently begins rubbing the ointment over her mother's sores.*

BRIGHTON enters from the main stairway. He glances around the room looking for TEDDY. He picks up the small suitcase)

BRIGHTON (*Calling towards TEDDY's room*) Teddy, I had this idea! I could pick up some biscuit dough on the way to the cottage.

(*He laughs with a snort*)

Teddy?! I've got your bag. I'll be down in the car.

(BRIGHTON *exits down the main stairway*)

JEN Are you leaving?

TEDDY Yes.

JEN Alright.

TEDDY Mama?

JEN What?

TEDDY I don't have a feeling anymore like it's never gonna get better.

JEN You don't?

TEDDY No.

JEN Why's that?

TEDDY It's like I can smell the rain coming and I can feel it's gonna start to thunder.

JEN It is? It's gonna thunder?

TEDDY Yeah, and that ole snapping turtle's gonna let loose and I'll just be standing there in the rain and in the thunder and these arms will want to hold onto somebody and have their arms holding onto me.

JEN Hmm. Well. I hope so. I, well, I . . . Yes. Good. Yes.

(TEDDY *continues putting on the ointment, as they both smoke cigarettes and the lights fade to blackout*)

END OF PLAY

Library of Congress Cataloging-in-Publication Data

Henley, Beth.

    The debutante ball / Beth Henley : with art by
Lynn Green Root.

       p.   cm. — (Author and artist series)

    ISBN 0-87805-543-6. — ISBN 0-87805-518-5
(limited ed.)

    I. Root, Lynn, 1954— . II. Title. III. Series.

PS3558.E4962D4   1991

812′.54—dc20   91-23878

                                 CIP